ULTIMATE BASS FISHING LIBRARY

HUNTING FOR TROPHY BASS

HOW AND WHERE TO CATCH
THE FISH OF A LIFETIME

MONTGOMERY, ALABAMA

INTRODUCTION
A Quest For Big Bass

O N June 2, 1932, an avid but meagerly equipped farmer named George W. Perry went fishing to catch food for his family dinner table. What he ended up catching from Georgia's Montgomery Lake was more than a meal.

After hours spent chunking and winding a Creek Chub Wiggle-Fish in the dark water of the tiny oxbow lake, the 19-year-old Perry eventually tied into what remains today the dream catch of every fanatical bass fisherman.

The story of how Perry tied into the 22-pound, 4-ounce world record largemouth reads like most ordinary big fish stories. He made a cast near a cypress log, twitched the topwater lure, and the surface exploded as the fish took the bait. Perry reared back and set the hook, but nothing budged. He thought for sure the fish had gotten away and the lure snagged in a limb. He was more worried about losing his lure at the time because he'd carried only two baits for the trip.

Then the "snag" began to move and the fight was on. The rest of the story is rather uneventful compared to how it would be treated today. The fish was weighed on certified scales, and Perry entered it into a *Field & Stream* fishing contest, winning its $75 bounty of outdoor gear. After filling out the contest application, Perry took the fish home, and the family made a hearty meal of it.

Today, the catch ranks as the most impressive angling record ever set — and the toughest to break. While the fish was food for Perry, the next record, if it is ever broken, could net the lucky angler $1 million or more from the tackle companies eager to claim the prize was caught using their gear.

In the meantime, the pursuit to break the record goes on. A small fraternity of world record hunters is centered in Southern California, where the record has come close to being broken. While they treat 10-pounders like a tournament fisherman does throwback dinks, the rest of the angling world is content just to break the double-digit mark as a milestone achievement.

Perry did not catch his record fish by honing in on the spot with a GPS receiver. Nor was he standing on the bow of a bass boat with a 200-hp outboard rigged to its stern. His rod and reel was so cheap, today's sophisticated bass fishermen would laugh at the rig.

But the fact of life today is that life is just not that simple anymore. Bass fishing takes careful strategizing and a host of high-tech tackle to make it fun. Or does it?

You be the judge. In the meantime, this book will help you in your quest to catch the double-digit prize that is your ultimate goal.

Copyright 2004 by BASS

Published in 2004 by BASS
5845 Carmichael Road
Montgomery, AL 36117

Editor In Chief:
Dave Precht

Editor:
James Hall

Managing Editor:
Craig Lamb

Editorial Assistant:
Althea Goodyear

Art Director:
Rick Reed

Designers:
Laurie Willis, Leah Cochrane,
Bill Gantt, Nancy Lavender

Illustrators:
Chris Armstrong, Shannon Barnes,
Lenny McPherson

Photography Manager:
Gerald Crawford

Contributing Writers:
Grady Allen, Richard Alden Bean,
Homer Circle, David Hart,
Bruce Ingram, Michael Jones,
Ronnie Kovach, Jay Kumar,
Bob McNally, John Neporadny Jr.,
Dave Precht, Steve Price, Paul Prorok,
Frank Sargeant, Ray Sasser, Louie Stout,
Tim Tucker, Don Wirth

Contributing Photographers:
Richard Alden Bean, Charles Beck,
Soc Clay, Gerald Crawford, James Hall,
David Hart, Bryan Hendricks,
Bruce Ingram, Michael Jones,
Bill Lindner, Bob McNally,
John Neporadny Jr., Dave Precht,
Steve Price, Paul Prorok, David Sams,
Ray Sasser, Doug Stamm,
Gary Tramontina, Tim Tucker, Don Wirth

Copy Editors:
Laura Harris, Debbie Salter

Manufacturing Manager:
Bill Holmes

Marketing:
Betsy B. Peters

**Vice President &
General Manager, BASS:**
Dean Kessel

Printed on American paper by
RR Donnelley

ISBN 1-890280-04-6

IF YOU ARE HAUNTED by thoughts of monster bass, fear not. The following pages will change the nightmare of missing a trophy into catching the bass of your dreams.

CONTENTS

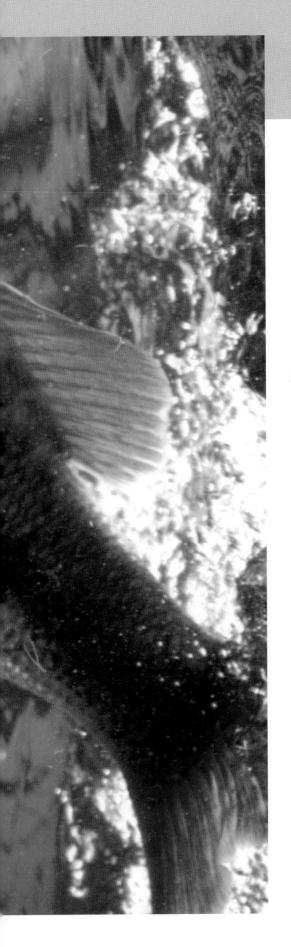

ALL ABOUT TROPHY BASS

Get into the mind of a lunker to catch this territorial loner . . .

AS THEY AGE and grow in size, big bass become loners and stake out a territory.

UNDERSTANDING TROPHY BASS BEHAVIOR

When a bass reaches 10 pounds, it becomes a different creature — a much warier creature

FOR EIGHT YEARS, Mike Long studied the movements of the same behemoth largemouth prowling the waters of California's Lake Poway. He grew to know it well, and literally, from inside and out.

Each fall and winter, when rainbow trout were being stocked, the big fish lived by boat docks near the ramp where trout were released. Each summer, when bass fishing pressure increased, the fish moved into an area where fishing was prohibited.

Long estimates the bass grew to a weight of 19 to 20 pounds during the time he followed it around the lake. And while the trophy specialist never caught that bass, he has landed 20 bass weighing in excess of 17 pounds. That includes a 20-12 he caught in April 2001.

Since Long began fishing specifically for trophy largemouth 12 years ago, he has caught 236 fish weighing more than 10 pounds — on 20 different lakes. That is an astounding and remarkable achievement, to say the very least.

What he gained from following the big fish on Lake Poway was an insight into the personality of monster bass — an insight the San Diego angler has come to realize is absolutely indispensable for anyone who hopes to catch trophy class largemouth on a regular basis.

(Opposite page) BASS PRO KELLY Jordon looks for subtle differences in otherwise ordinary places. That makes fishing slowly and keeping the lure on the bottom the key to finding such irregularities.

"You can never say bass behave uniformly anywhere or anytime," says Long, "but I can assure you, big bass are totally different fish from smaller ones. At some point — when it reaches a certain age or weight, or both — the personality of a big bass changes. I firmly believe the

key to catching them once they do reach that size is learning as much as you can about that personality change."

Long is not alone in believing trophy bass undergo a distinct behavioral change. Fellow San Diego big bass expert Bill Murphy concurs, as do experienced biologists, guides and trophy bass fishermen in Texas and Florida, two other states that regularly produce "teen" bass.

Murphy, who has caught several bass over 17 pounds, believes this change begins when the bass

reaches a weight between 8 and 9 pounds. He equates this transformation from juvenile to adult to the way humans mature to adulthood — only it happens more quickly with bass.

"Big bass change depth, they change cover and they change eating habits," explains Murphy. "Big bass also become much more cautious, and I believe they establish a routine in which even the slightest change might upset them. And, of course, when they're upset, you're not likely to catch them."

"One of the first things I noticed about big bass is that for the most part, they're loners," adds Long. "These fish become very territorial — probably because they're big enough to rule a specific domain. That territory is also going to be a prime spot. It will not necessarily be very large, but it will have quick access to deeper water and easy access to food or a feeding area.

"I believe these are two of the most important considerations for any fisherman who wants to catch big bass: Understand what the bass are eating, and learn where they're staying."

Long's observations and experiences have shown him that big bass spend much of their time right on the bottom, at least until sunlight levels are reduced. Only then do the fish really move into shallower zones, and they do not often remain shallow long.

"Big bass truly love steep edges and channels," he says. "That's probably for security as much as anything. Big bass are very wary, and depth offers the fastest, most secure route to safety. I regularly see huge bass in 30 to 40 feet of water. Even though the 20-pound, 12-ounce bass I caught this spring was spawning in 8 to 10 feet of water, her nest was only a few yards away from a drop down to about 80 feet.

"During the late summer here, many of us fish with topwater lures in shallow water, and we all catch a number of fish in the 8-pound range. Very, very seldom, however, do we catch one of the really big bass that shallow. Except in the spring."

Kelly Jordon, a veteran Lake Fork, Texas, guide and BASS pro who has caught more than 50 bass weighing over 10 pounds, notes that virtually all his fish heavier than 10 pounds came from water an average of 4 or 5 feet deeper than the depths from which he has caught smaller bass. Even during the spring, when bass move shallow to spawn, smaller fish will be in water 2 to 4 feet deep, while larger bass are using 7- to 10-foot depths.

"We can actually follow the big bass on Lake Fork to some extent through the spawn and postspawn," explains Jordon. "There's a magic window of time in May when the big bass are moving toward deep water, and we catch quite a few between 18 and 25 feet.

"After that, we lose them. Below 25 feet on Fork, the availability of structure is reduced, and the fish apparently scatter. Statistically, few really big bass are caught on Fork during the summer, because it's so difficult to define a specific structure feature they might be using."

In addition to being on slightly deeper structure, the largest fish will homestead the very best part of that structure, according to experienced big bass anglers. It isn't enough to simply find a sharp drop or breakline — you have to study it for additional features. These subtle differences may not show up on depthfinder screens.

"Most of the time, you find these features by fishing," says Jordon. "You crawl your worm or hop your jig along the bottom, and suddenly it hits a snag. A lone tree or a little pile of rocks might be the real key. This is another reason fishing slowly and keeping your bait on the bottom is beneficial. You have to pay attention, because your lures are your eyes and ears down there."

Jordon has noticed that all his big bass have come from areas where baitfish are abundant. He has learned over the years that big bass appear to develop a distinct preference for certain species of forage, and they even seem to ignore other species that might be easier for them to catch. On Fork, the year-round favorite foods for big bass are crappie and yellow bass.

"The Texas state record bass (18.18 pounds) was caught in a classic deep water crappie hole on Fork, by Barry St. Clair, who was crappie fishing at the time." Adding to that predator theory is a scenario encountered by Jordon, who caught a 12-pounder after locating a huge concentration of yellow bass in 35 feet of water. He spotted the yellow bass with his depthfinder and began jigging a spoon beneath the massive school; 10 minutes later he brought up the big bass.

"I think big bass stake out a home in a spot where the food they really prefer is easy to find,"

Creed of the Trophy Hunter

Ordinary bass are caught by ordinary fishermen, but to fish deliberately for trophy bass is the earmark of a specialist. He lives to bass-fish, knows their favored hangouts, has ways to approach them differently than the ordinary fisherman and understands what makes them strike artificial lures.

Most fishermen settle for the common belief that bass take lures because they are hungry. This is only one of the seven reasons believed to cause trophy bass to blast artificial lures. Remember them, because any one could be the key to that bass of your lifetime:

■ **Hunger** — This is logical, because that's why humans eat. And when you find a school of lunkers in a feeding frenzy, it's a ball. But if this were the only reason, you would catch far fewer big bass.

■ **Greed** — Imagine this scenario. A small bass moves in behind a lure, tails it, but is bluffed out by a big bass that charges in to engulf the lure. As the lure is removed from the bass' mouth, the tail of a minnow protrudes from its throat. The impulse was greed more than hunger.

■ **Gluttony** — Bass are commonly observed in a feeding frenzy, with bulging stomachs and minnows in their maws. Yet they keep on gorging shiners. As some are landed, minnows spew out of their jaws. This suggests gluttonous gorging.

■ **Protective instinct** — When a bass is guarding a nest of eggs or a brood of hatchlings and a lure intrudes, the female grabs the lure, crushes it, swims away from the nest and blows it out. There is no attempt to eat the lure.

■ **Curiosity** — When a big bass follows closely behind your lure several times but doesn't take it, this shows a lack of hunger. One trick that sometimes takes these bass is next.

■ **Reflexive action** — When a burly bass tails your lure, try reeling very rapidly, stop it suddenly, then fast-reel again, triggering reflexive grabs. For example, if I were to suddenly toss you a ball for no reason, you would reflexively grab it.

■ **Territoriality** — Big bass are very territorial, resenting any critter daring to invade. If you see a big bass cruising a certain area, repeatedly cast a big lure at it. It may take more than a dozen casts to arouse it, but what vicious blasts!

Jordon says. "This might be on the sharp drop at the edge of a flat or wide point, or it may be along a migration route the forage uses regularly. Once in a while, big bass go on a feeding binge like smaller bass, but most of the time big bass do not expend a lot of energy chasing bait or lures."

"You have to remember that as a bass grows older and larger, its metabolism slows," points out Long. "This slowdown must occur over a fairly short period in the fish's life, too, or maybe it's part of this personality change. Anyway, I have caught big bass when my lures were lying completely motionless on the bottom, and so have other fishermen. It's not an accident. The bass don't go very far or want to work very hard for their meals."

What all this means is that most successful trophy bass pros catch the majority of their fish by working their lures extra-slow and close to the bottom. The most dedicated California anglers realize this type of fishing might result in only one or two strikes a day, but they're willing to wait for that chance.

The popular saying that big bass like big lures is very true, and may also relate to the metabolism change. Long and many other California anglers regularly catch some of their biggest bass on the famous "swim baits" — imitation trout in sizes as long as 12 inches.

"What's very interesting," adds Long, "is how big bass can become conditioned to a regular food source, such as the stocking of rainbow trout we have in many California lakes. After awhile, they seem to know when the trout truck is due to arrive, and they begin showing up around the docks before the trucks arrive.

"In many instances, the stockings are two weeks apart, but the fish somehow seem to recognize this. They're not around during the off-week. I've done studies on this at Poway, Dixon and Jennings (three San Diego area lakes), and the behavior of the bass is basically the same.

"I can't explain that, except to think that somehow the fish have an internal clock that guides their behavior. Sometimes you see this in other wildlife, and it is evident in the way a pet dog will sit by the front door at 5:30 p.m., waiting for its owner to come home from work. I think it's really fascinating."

Increased wariness also becomes part of the lifestyle of a big bass, declares Long. Creel studies by California fisheries biologists have shown that catch rates of trophy bass fluctuate considerably

between weekdays and weekends. Long's solution is to fish on weekdays or foul weather days, when fewer anglers are on the water.

"There is an area on Lake Dixon (the lake where Long caught his 20-12) we call 'Trout Cove,'" says Long, "and I used to watch a big bass there that stayed under a boat dock. You could see her there early in the morning before anyone arrived, but as soon as people began walking on the dock, that bass would move 50 yards away, to the edge of a deep drop.

"On a rainy, dreary day when no one came out on the dock, she'd just stay there."

Adds Murphy, "Big bass don't argue with you. They just swim away. They're so in tune with their environment, they can instantly detect any change in their surroundings.

"This is especially true of fishing lures that come crashing down into their little territory. I've seen this as a scuba diver. I'd go down to a spot where I'd see a big bass, and, of course, it would just slowly swim away. If I sat down very quietly on the bottom and did not move, eventually the fish would return."

The lessons here for big bass hunters are simply to be quiet and, especially, patient. The fish know anglers are present long before anglers know fish are present. When Long caught his giant, his swim bait had actually been almost completely stationary in the water for an hour, and he was so far away he couldn't see his bait or the fish. It took that long for the big bass to finally come back to the lure.

"When I talk to people about trophy bass fishing, I tell them to be patient and fish deep," emphasizes Long. "And then I tell them to fish deep and be patient.

"There's no question that when you go after a really big bass, you're dealing with a different type of fish — one whose personality is not at all like the smaller bass you're accustomed to catching."

BIG BASS develop a distinct appetite for a certain species of forage. In western lakes, they prefer stocked rainbow trout; in other lakes it might be crappie or perch.

A SYSTEMATIC APPROACH FOR BIG BASS

To catch heavyweight bass consistently, follow these seven steps to success

BIG BASS. We've all heard that phrase. But it has relative meaning, depending on where one fishes.

For example, near the town of Alexandria in west-central Minnesota, a big bass is 4 or 5 pounds. But a bass that size does not raise an eyebrow on Bull Shoals Reservoir in northern Arkansas. There, it takes a 6- or 7-pounder to get any kind of attention.

And in the Deep South, 8 pounds is the magic number, unless you live in Florida or California, where 10 pounds is the hallmark of a real bass.

It's a complicated subject, this notion of big fish, but it's one that concerns bass anglers everywhere.

This brings up an important point: It takes more than luck to catch big bass.

You can set out to get your trophy and be successful, if you go by the following systematic approach to catching a lunker.

1. DEFINE WHAT 'BIG' IS

To target big bass, an angler first must determine what big means. Locale and species govern the maximum size bass can attain. If the target bass is a 3-pound Canadian smallmouth, or a 4-pound Alabama spotted bass, or a 12-pound Florida largemouth, then so be it. But to catch such a fish, the fisherman has to determine in his own mind what that fish must weigh to qualify as big in the locale he has chosen to catch it.

Once the size of the bass sought is determined, an angler then can begin a determined, systematic process to catch it.

2. KNOW THE HIDING PLACES

The next step to catching a big bass is to learn the most likely places to find one. Since all bass water is not equally productive, it's imperative for anglers to do plenty of research to identify where they should spend the bulk of their fishing hours.

Too many fishermen automatically assume that the biggest, most popular and best-known lakes offer the best chances for catching big bass. But the odds are that such an assumption is false.

Many waters well-known for their big bass have a tremendous amount of fishing pressure, and so are not as good for trophy bass fishing as catch reports might lead one to believe. For example, a few Florida lakes have gained worldwide notoriety for giving up huge numbers of 10-pound largemouth.

The lakes still produce about the same number of big bass as they did decades ago, but 10 times the number of anglers fish them to produce the same number of big bass. So, the odds of an angler catching a true trophy from such a lake are much less than they were a generation ago. Interestingly, a lesser-known lake only 15 minutes from the famous one can be a much better spot to catch a 10-pound bass. The lake is much smaller, receives comparatively little fishing pressure, and the ratio of angling man-hours per trophy fish landed is much better than on a famous lake.

The lake is simply overlooked by the legions of anglers who rush headlong to the well-known hot spot because they believe it is the only place worth fishing for big bass.

One of the best sources for information on prime big bass water is from state fisheries department personnel. A tremendous amount of

information can be garnered from biologists and fisheries managers, as they are on the water all the time, doing research, making creel surveys and tagging fish.

Local newspaper outdoor writers also can put anglers on to hot spots for big bass. Most good outdoor writers keep abreast of the best bass lakes, and many know some not-so-well-known sleeper spots. Bait and tackle shops, fishing-camp owners, and even guides can be extremely helpful.

Regarding guides, be sure to talk to several good ones who are very familiar with the waters you want to fish. Outdoor writers, fisheries department personnel or similar people who have nothing to gain personally by making recommendations should recommend guides.

When speaking with guides, tell them you're only interested in big fish, a personal trophy for yourself. Explain you want the fish for mounting, or possibly just a photograph before releasing it. If you like the guide, and his answers to your questions are sincere, hire the man for a day or two to try specifically for big fish the way he prefers to get them. You can learn more about a lake, its trophy fish, and how to catch them during a two day guide trip than you can in a month on your own.

3. THINK OUTSIDE THE BOX

Do your own exploring. Sometimes the very best big bass waters are so small, underrated or overlooked, that virtually no one fishes them, and even fisheries biologists have no inkling what the

THE ODDS of catching a trophy bass are higher on "no-name" lakes located near popular fisheries that get hammered by the masses.

little lakes contain. In this case, you have no other choice than to explore and test them on your own.

Often you can tell a lot about a lake just by looking at it. If the place has at least some deep water (6 or 8 feet is minimum, and 10 to 15 feet is better); some broad, shallow flats with weedbeds, brushpiles or similar cover; and limited development nearby, it's well worth fishing.

Many of the best lakes have a lot of wildlife along their shores, such as herons, kingfishers, gulls, ospreys, raccoons, turtles and the like. It takes a fertile lake to sustain such wildlife, and if it does, it's likely that big bass abound, too.

Extensive development around a lake turns off a lot of anglers, but it can be deceiving in determining a lake's potential. Golf courses and homes built around small lakes are a prime example. Because they are rarely fished, these hidden jewels can produce double-digit bass. Such is the case in Florida, where the growing season for bass is virtually year-round.

Borrow pits, farm ponds, oxbow lakes, city park lakes and lagoons, and even roadside canals and ditches all can harbor the bass of an angler's trophy dreams. Only by keeping your eyes and ears open at all times will you get tips on such waters, and only by checking them out yourself will you learn if big fish are present.

4. GET TO KNOW THE HAUNTS

Learn your waters well. It should be noted here that once you've targeted several good waters you're sure hold a healthy population of the trophy bass you seek, stick with them. Spend time learning everything there is to know about those very few, well-chosen, trophy bass waters. On those lakes and rivers, spend enough time to know where the deep water is, where there are spawning flats and bays, where the dropoffs are, where sunken brushpiles and logs lie and where there is structure.

Take note of the primary bass forage and where

it's most plentiful. Only by thoroughly learning such things about a lake, and by fishing it constantly, can you have complete confidence that you can catch the trophy bass that exist there.

5. TIMING IS EVERYTHING

Go at the right time. Timing is an important part to a systematic approach to catching big bass. Simply stated, an angler should be on the water when the time is right for catching heavyweights. This means avoiding cold front conditions; fishing at the peak times of day, such as daybreak, dusk and at night during summer, and during warming trends in the spring and fall.

These times also can vary dramatically on different waters. For example, if the river that you know is jammed with big smallmouth but is a washout in spring because of runoff, don't beat your head against a wall trying to fish it then. Locate some lakes or other streams that are not so vulnerable to rain. Work the river when it's the proper time to do so.

It takes a conscious effort to be on the water at the right times when the biggest trophy bass are on the prowl and looking for an easy meal. But this effort is well worth the trouble.

6. WITH LURES, THINK BIG

Use big bass lures. It may sound like an old saw to many veteran anglers, but big fish are most easily duped into hitting big lures rather than small ones. This is a general rule, naturally, because large bass are caught daily on small lures. But a stout bass lives basically on the expended-energy principle.

That is, a fish will not expend more energy to catch forage than that forage provides in nutritional value. What that means in regard to lure selection is that a large bass is most likely to take a large plastic worm, a big spinnerbait or an oversize topwater plug than it is to take tiny, ultralight models of the same lure.

The same goes for live bait. Big shiners, soft-shell crawfish and heavy water dogs are much more likely to tempt a largemouth bass into hitting than would a tiny crappie minnow.

7. DEVELOP AN ATTITUDE

Finally, it's important that anyone who seeks big bass assume a big fish attitude. He must settle for nothing less than his goal, and it's of paramount importance that he have complete dedication to those ambitions.

It's a determination that can be likened in many ways to a trophy deer hunter. The sportsman who hunts nothing but big bucks will not settle for anything less. He is 100 percent committed to getting a buck with a massive rack, or he will shoot no deer at all.

Trophy bass hunters, too, must share that mental attitude regarding trophy fish. Settle for nothing less than your big bass goal, and it's likely you'll attain the prize of your angling dreams.

BE SPECIFIC when on the hunt for a trophy. Go at the right time, use big baits and think outside the box.

FISHING TROPHY WATERS

To catch the trophy of your dreams, you need to know where to look . . .

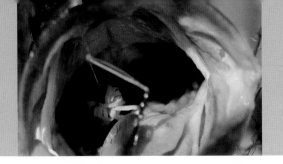

GIANT BASS AND THE STRUCTURE CONNECTION

A noted trophy bass expert discusses bottom structure and other factors that attract huge bass

CURRENT WISDOM HOLDS THAT THE PLACE TO CATCH a giant bass is in a Southern California lake. The large-growing Florida strain of largemouth was first stocked in the San Diego Lakes in 1959, and their descendants now are pushing world record weight.

Several California anglers in recent years have become obsessed with catching a new world record. They have developed precise strategies for finding and fooling a bass weighing more than 22 pounds, 4 ounces, the standing world record. Some have come close, including Bob Crupi, whose 22.04-pounder in 1990 is the second-largest bass of all time.

Among the giant bass hunters, few know more about the habits and peculiarities of Florida largemouth than Bill Murphy, who has spent the past three decades fishing and learning everything he can about these huge fish. His hard-won lessons should help bass anglers everywhere in their own quests for trophy bass.

THE RIGHT SPOT

Like most savvy bass anglers, Murphy recognizes that every lake has a key — key spot, key presentation, key color, etc. And finding the keys in every situation is

BILL MURPHY has his best success on structure that drops off in three directions, like a long point bordered by an erosion ditch.

(Opposite page) SOUTHERN CALIFORNIA trophy hunter Bill Murphy finds that everything tends to move deeper as it gets bigger — both bass and their prey.

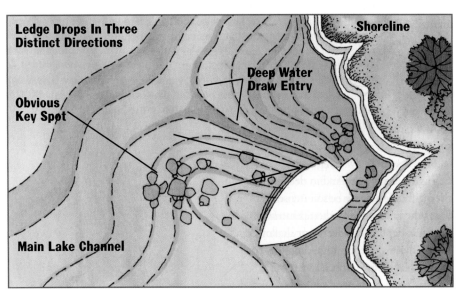

Ledge Drops In Three Distinct Directions

Shoreline

Deep Water Draw Entry

Obvious Key Spot

Main Lake Channel

something traveling tournament fishermen understand well. Anglers who travel extensively and fish a variety of waters have to find the key, unique characteristics that govern how bass react on each fishery.

"Giant bass appear elusive because, in reality, only few spots attract them. True lunker bass only gravitate to spots with certain ingredients," he believes. "In smaller lakes, or smaller sections of larger lakes, there may only be one or two spots in the entire area that consistently attract lunkers."

For example, a creek arm may have 10 clearly defined channel bends, with half of them holding small fish but only one or two offering trophy bass potential. The bends that do attract trophy fish will be the most consistent spots in the entire creek arm, Murphy reasons. On days when activity is high, these super spots could produce limits of big fish. And even when activity is low, these spots may yield a few nice bass when all other channel bends are empty.

"Once you become familiar with the key elements that make a structure a prime big bass structure, you can use this backlog of knowledge to locate potential trophy areas wherever you fish," he adds.

BIG BASS tend to follow ditches or "draws" to and from feeding zones. Consequently, Bill Murphy believes these fish rarely cross shallow structure.

OUTER EDGE SPOTS

Changing the focus from shallow water to deeper zones is the first step to catching lunker bass in lakes with structure environments, and Murphy says this is especially important in lakes that receive heavy fishing pressure.

"When bass reach 4 pounds or larger, they begin to lose the habits of smaller bass and take on the characteristics of adults," he reasons. "One of the most obvious changes upon reaching adulthood is a shift in location from shallow habitats to outer edges close to deep water."

Everything tends to move deeper as it gets bigger — both bass and their prey. An adult body allows a large bass to utilize larger prey that can't be exploited by small bass.

Besides providing excellent feeding opportunities, deep water is a place where the biggest bass find security. Through the years, Murphy has found that shallow cover may be the most secure habitat for yearlings, but a large adult bass can use the vast expanses of deep, open water to disappear at the first hint of danger.

The trophy bass expert notes the connection between deep, open water, and security is so strong in adults that the biggest bass will not use a spot unless deep water is so close the fish can move deeper with just a swish of its tail.

"When I say that big bass are deep water oriented, I don't want to imply that all big bass are always near deep water," he cautions. "Adult fish are individuals, and there are always some big bass that live up on shallow flats and along shallow shorelines where small bass predominantly live. But in lakes having deeper zones with adequate bottom structure and food sources, it has been my experience that the biggest bass will most likely be found around the outside edges of structural features like underwater bars, humps, rockpiles, reefs and dropoffs."

Of course, deep is a relative term, and only a foot or two of depth change can be

extremely important in some lakes. But whether a spot breaks from 10 feet into 12 feet, or from 40 feet down to 70 feet, Murphy has found the relationship remains the same.

"Another truism I find about structured lakes is that trophy bass like structures near a main channel or main lake basin that contains the deepest water in the area," continues Murphy.

The key areas on prime big bass structures are the outer perimeters close to deeper water, and the key features along the outer perimeter is the edge of a sharp dropoff separating deep water from the shallows. Murphy's experience indicates that bass may suspend far off structure over open water, or move up onto the shallowest part of a structure, but the outer edges are the pivot points of big bass activity.

Murphy describes an ideal big bass spot as an outer edge that breaks off in two or three different directions. A dropoff that runs straight, without ir-

regularities, isn't as attractive (big bass rarely use straight breaklines, unless they are the only option, or unless overcrowding on more desirable structure causes some fish to use secondary spots).

Look for combinations of edge spots wherever deep water access points come together: where a channel connects with a deep basin, a stream cut or erosion cut intersects a channel, or where two channels meet. Any place where deep features come together always has big fish potential.

TIMING IS ALMOST EVERYTHING

Murphy believes that one reason trophy bass are so seldom caught is because feeding periods of large bass vary significantly from feeding patterns of small bass. Like kids growing up, bass under 4 pounds require food constantly and are likely to feed at any time throughout the day — and their willingness to bite makes them easier targets.

"Big bass, however, tend to eat a lot at one

BILL MURPHY preaches that big bass are deep water creatures. In shallow lakes, however, the fish will congregate around outside edges of structural features, like weedy points.

Murphy's Laws

Over the years and especially through his recent writing, Bill Murphy has expressed some maverick opinions about bass and bass fishing. Some fly in the face of prevailing wisdom — most are thought-provoking.

Here's a sample:

■ On Florida bass — "Floridas are a different fish with different habits, and this fact made them hard to catch for most people. When Floridas were first introduced, they acted like bass back in Florida — they kept their shallow water instincts. For example, at the same time native bass related to dropoffs at 22 feet, Florida bass could be found in heavy cover, sometimes so shallow we had to fish from the bank to reach places inaccessible to boats."

■ On oxygen and bass — "If a spot has no oxygen, obviously, bass won't be there, but a spot doesn't have to have textbook parts-per-million to be tolerable to a big bass. Everyone thinks of comfort in terms of oxygen content and temperature, but for giant bass, security is often the most important comfort factor. The most comfortable spot for a big bass is a preferred structural feature with the security of deep, open water nearby, even if it is slightly lower in oxygen."

■ On water temperature and bass — "Water temperature is another myth. People are always looking for some magic correlation, but big bass fishing is too complex to make it so simplified. You can't say that bass will be at a certain place just because it's a certain time of year, or because the water is a certain temperature. Big bass stay in certain places because that's where they live. Security and food sources are the factors that override everything to the largest bass."

■ On live bait — "Changing conditions are more apt to hinder the bite on artificial lures, but live bait may appeal to bass regardless of conditions! I've always been a firm believer that if you put the right live bait in front of a bass, it will often bite even during periods with bad influences. Big bass love wild shiners, and there's no way around this fact."

■ On bass studies — "From a pure angling perspective, the only way to evaluate what bass do is by hook and line. You can't study them in an aquarium because a captive animal doesn't have the same attitude as it does in the wild. You can't examine them under water, because as soon as they see you, your presence influences their habits. When you put a transmitter into a fish, who's to say it doesn't influence its normal behavior? The only way to study big bass is to fish for them."

■ On intuition — "Once you learn how bass live in their world, your intuition will begin to direct you in successful ways. And in the sport of big bass fishing, you just have to trust that some things are true; you can't prove it, so you just have to believe. But if you believe in something and it works — who cares if it's correct?"

BAROMETRIC PRESSURE influences big bass behavior more than actual weather changes, like pre-frontal conditions.

At one point, however, a peak period stimulates lunker fish to move, and you catch three 5-pounders and a 9-pounder in only 20 minutes. The big fish movement might consist of a small group or just one lunker, but in either case, the short time in which fish actually feed, or visit the structure, makes timing especially critical.

Because proper timing is so important, it's possible for a skilled angler to fish for years and never contact a true lunker bass if he fails to be at the right spot during one of these short feeding sprees, and this fact goes double on heavily fished waters. You have to make every effort to be on the water when the big fish are most active and catchable.

Normally, the exact time of the daily active period is impossible to predict in advance, but certain keys in nature can direct you to certain spots at certain times.

"Old-timers used to say that bass fishing was better early in the morning and late in the evening, but that philosophy was based on the fact that most fishermen back then only worked shorelines — where fishing is often best early and late," adds Murphy.

time, taking what they need all at once, then settling down and conserving energy," he says. "A typical feeding pattern for large bass in a 24-hour period would be a flurry of activity of a fairly short duration, followed by long periods if inactivity."

In deep water structure fishing, early and late can also be good, but one of the very best trophy bass periods is from 10 a.m. until 2 p.m. By late morning, as the sun continues to heat the earth, subtle changes in air temperature, humidity and wind direction can prompt prime active periods during midday hours.

PREFRONTAL CONDITIONS

The fact that big bass bite best on the front side of an approaching frontal system and least on the back side is a truism anglers discover wherever they fish for bass.

While most anglers credit overcast prefrontal conditions for prompting good fishing and bright, cloudless, postfrontal weather for causing bass to shut off, Murphy's studies point to barometric pressure as having a more important influence on big bass activity.

"We like to blame the clear skies and cool temperatures following a cold front for bad fishing, but rather than a limiting factor in themselves, these conditions signal a change in barometric pressure," he says.

"As the cold front approaches and the barometric pressure falls, big bass bite well. But after the front moves through and the barometric pressure begins to rise, conditions become cool and clear, and the bigger fish shut off," he continues. "Everyone likes to finger the weather, but I believe the change in barometric pressure is the real culprit."

Reverse the conditions and this philosophy comes into focus. The same bright, cloudless sky that people blame for poor fishing can be excellent when it occurs prior to an approaching frontal system.

"One of the best days I've ever had was when an approaching front had stalled a day or so away and the cloud cover hadn't yet arrived," he relates. "The sun was intense and burning, but the bass were stimulated by the falling barometric pressure and bit like crazy. I caught a bass 7 pounds or bigger on almost every cast for over an hour."

Barometric pressure is the real cause of big bass activity. Air temperature, cloud cover and wind direction are only symptoms of a larger pressure system.

One fact that is often ignored about bad fishing after a front is that most of the fish are already full and satisfied, according to Murphy. Just before the front, and possibly for several days before the front, the falling barometric pressure caused the bigger fish to go on a wild feeding spree. But on the next day after the front goes through, conditions got bright and clear and you couldn't "buy" a fish.

What happens is that almost every fish in the lake has completely gorged itself, and after the front they won't feed. A few lunker fish for some reason may not have fed well during the frenzy and might still be caught, but generally not many.

"A prefrontal influence with a falling barometer is the most consistent big bass pattern I know. When the barometer begins to change, nature is telling you something is happening, and it's time to get serious," he says. "Lock into a key outside structure and fish it hard, even if the same spot hasn't produced just a short time before. Conditions are changing, and big fish may be ready to move in. Make every effort to be in the right spot at the right time — a prefrontal condition is the most reliable big fish pattern there is."

THE FRONT MAY be miles away, but the big fish will turn on as the barometer falls, even in bluebird skies.

LUNKER BASS TIME ON WATER SUPPLY LAKES

These small reservoirs can be dynamite in the transition period from winter to spring

THE TIME IS LATE WINTER — specifically that period when the daytime air temperature consistently rises into the mid to upper 30s, but still before that eagerly anticipated period when the temperature will dare to daily top the 40 degree barrier.

Bill Nease is slowly motoring across a water supply lake near his Martinsville, Va., home. Nease has the lake, which is considerably less than 100 acres, all to himself. And it's not hard to understand why.

Conventional wisdom has it that heavily fished water supply impoundments receive too much pressure to produce big bass. And even those who

want to catch keeper-size bass, or just enjoy getting out, know that both the fishing and boating will be more enjoyable in several weeks.

Nease has already fished for three hours with only one strike to show for his efforts. But then, the avid outdoorsman perceives his line twitch, and a few minutes later he lands and releases an 8 1/2-pound largemouth. Nease continues to fish for another four hours, coaxing only two more bites from the lake's bass. He fails to connect on one of the strikes, but the other results in a 6-pounder coming aboard.

After a long day on the water, the angler returns home, very pleased with his efforts. The fact that there were no witnesses doesn't bother him a bit.

Just why does this big bass addict visit water supply lakes when nationally known impoundments such as Smith Mountain and Buggs Island are close to his home?

"That's a fair question," Nease says with a laugh. "Actually, for most of the year, water supply lakes — at least the ones I fish — are terrible places to catch big fish, or even a limit of keepers. Water supply lakes receive tremendous fishing and boating pressure from spring through fall. And I think that's probably true with water supply lakes around the country.

"Many, if not most, of the bass caught are kept, and the few that are let go become very wary. The fishing is made even more difficult because once early spring arrives, fishermen have to share these small lakes with pleasure boaters and, later in the season, with skiers and swimmers."

The very nature of water supply lakes increases the angling difficulty, continues Nease. Very clear water, steep sides, a lack of shoreline cover, limited forage species and flat, relatively featureless bottoms characterize many water supply reservoirs. These lakes often are small (typically less than 100 acres), and their angling "secrets" and best spots are well-known.

But there is a very brief window of opportunity on these impoundments when they can produce trophy bass. That's when Nease, who has caught largemouth up to 11 pounds, 11 ounces from water supply lakes, targets these bodies of water.

"There is a very short period of time, about two weeks, when these little lakes are awesome places to fish," he says. "In late winter, when the water first begins to warm and the bass first start to move up from deep water, those big fish are catchable. They haven't seen a lure in a long time, and they are looking for a meal.

"If an angler waits until those big bass go on their beds, he's waited too long. By then, everybody and his brother will be tossing lures and live bait to those fish, and they will be very spooky. And the boating pressure will have picked up, too. It doesn't take too many boats to roil up a 30-acre reservoir."

Even during this prime time, anglers should not expect to catch many bass. Nease has never caught more than five bass on any late winter outing. Typically, water supply impoundments possess poor forage bases — often just crawfish, a

DON'T WAIT too long to fish a water supply lake. By spawning time, these small fisheries will be overwhelmed with angling pressure.

WATER SUPPLY LAKE guru Bill Nease will work shoreline cover in late winter, but only if a laydown extends into deep water.

few minnow species and bluegill. Given this condition, these lakes simply will not contain large populations of bass.

But there also have been times when the fish Nease caught averaged better than 5 pounds. One of the good things about the scarcity of bass on water supply reservoirs is that the few fish available are often quite large.

Nease's trophy tactics for water supply impoundments are not predicated upon fishing for bedding bass along the shoreline. Again, if an angler waits until the spawn to seek out these sows, he will have intense competition from other fishermen.

"I look for those transitional places where bass first congregate after they leave the midlake area and before they reach the bank," he says. "The best kind of cover for these places is wood. That wood might be a submerged log, little pieces of driftwood, a brushpile or just about anything."

Ideally, that wood should be situated where the water is just a

Sunken Christmas tree

8-12 feet of water

Brushpile on slight drop

Sparse wood cover

Laydown extending into deep water

Area slightly deeper than surrounding area

2 feet of water

Shoreline

PRIME TRANSITIONAL areas for largemouth on water supply impoundments are few. Nease repeatedly visits them over the course of a late winter day in the hope that some bass have moved to them from deep water.

Tips for Water Reservoirs

Bill Nease's lure choices are simple and traditional for water supply lakes. If the water is dingy, he employs a 1/4-ounce black or black/blue jig with a 900 series Uncle Josh pork spring lizard in the same colors. If the water is merely stained, the Virginian opts for a 1/4-ounce brown jig with a brown 800 series spring lizard. The 1/4-ounce size falls very slowly — a key at this time of year, when hits often occur as a bait descends. A major plus of the pork lizard is that its tail rides up, maintains Nease.

Other tools of the trade include 25-pound-test monofilament line for off-color water, 20-pound test for stained or clear liquid, a high gear ratio baitcasting reel, and a 6 1/2-foot Fenwick medium casting rod. Nease expresses very strong reasons for his choices.

"Jigs are standard baits for big bass and cold water," he says. "Just make sure the jig doesn't have rattles, which I think make the bait 'feel unnatural.' Besides, a jig being dragged over wood doesn't need any extra sound because it makes plenty of its own. Also, make sure the jig has a very wide gap hook that will be better able to penetrate a bass' mouth.

"In dingy water, fishermen may have to make five or six casts to every bit of wood cover before a strike will happen. I like to move the jig very slowly and then let it drop when I feel the bait rub against wood. I also recommend working the jig almost all the way back to the boat.

"In clearer water, I may make only two or three casts to wood, and I try to hit only the best spots. I also keep the jig moving all the time, and quickly reel it back in once the bait has left the cover."

The high speed reel and long rod are also very important. Nease says many late winter largemouth will engulf a jig and swim toward deep water. Before the angler settled on a rod and reel choice, he often ended up setting the hook when he had 6 or 7 feet of slack line out. Too frequently, the result was a poorly hooked trophy bass wallowing on the surface and flinging the hook. A high speed reel and long rod allows him to take up line quickly and set the hook with authority before a bass moves too far.

Bill Nease's big bass pattern takes place at a time when few people fish, and on a type of lake that most serious trophy fishermen ignore. Those two facts, however, may just be reasons enough for lunker chasers to implement his game plan on water supply lakes near their homes.

BILL NEASE believes serious trophy fishermen ignore water supply lakes, making them prime targets during the early fishing season.

little bit deeper than the surrounding areas; even a foot or so of extra depth is significant. Remember, emphasizes Nease, engineers do not design water supply impoundments for fishermen, and anglers should not expect to find vast expanses of wood cover or precipitous dropoffs. For reservoir creators to have left cover or features such as those would have been "inefficient."

Instead, anglers should look for small, seemingly insignificant pockets of slightly deeper water. A contour map and a depthfinder are indispensable tools for these mini-impoundments.

Occasionally, adds Nease, he will find jumbo bass along the shorelines. This situation typically occurs if a laydown extends into deep water. The most consistent patterns, though, are found in deep water.

Ideally, BASS members should look for favorable frontal conditions. Nease prefers a warming trend of any kind, even if that means a few days with air temperatures in the 30s when the previous week saw temperatures never rising above the upper 20s.

Finally, he favors slightly stained water over clear or muddy conditions. But he warns that the period when these bass are both unpressured and willing to bite is so brief that anglers can't afford to be overly picky. If you have a free afternoon to go fishing, take advantage of it.

DOWNSIZING FOR FARM POND LUNKERS

These pond fishing experts say small waters are the best bets for lifetime trophies

MOST TOURNAMENT BASS ANGLERS PREFER BIG WATERS. They consider sprawling lakes and reservoirs challenging to fish and conducive to limit catches of keepers. Plus, where else might these anglers get the chance to run their bass boats full-throttle?

But when it comes to bass waters, it's the other end of the scale that pulls the most weight. One of the great truths in bass fishing is that big bass thrive in small ponds. It is here, usually on private land, that bass can stretch the limits of their size potential.

Farm ponds are highly regarded as lunker factories. Every year, some of the biggest largemouth are taken from some minuscule fisheries — ponds whose primary reason for existing is to supply water for livestock or irrigation.

But how can you tell a true lunker pond from one that might only produce stunted bass? How can you gain access to fish these gems? And once you're there, what are the best lures and approaches to employ?

In reality, the same tactics that produce on a megaimpoundment like Toledo Bend will work on fish from Old McDonald's Pond. Concurrently, farm pond anglers are a special breed, willing to depart from angling conventions for a shot at the bass of a lifetime.

(Opposite page) SOME FARM ponds are, in theory, small lakes. A boat can give you a distinct advantage over shoreline anglers who can't get to prime offshore cover.

FORMULA FOR SUCCESS

Fisheries biologist Chris Stephenson is a full-time pond consultant in Alabama. He helps farmers and others who have ponds and small lakes to realize the maximum potential from their waters in terms of fish production.

"The most common form of pond management is directed at 'trophy' or jumbo bluegill," Stephenson says. "It may seem hard for readers to believe, but not every pond owner cares about growing 10-pound bass. As a consultant, I must first evaluate the pond, discern which management direction the owner desires, then proceed with an action plan to accomplish that goal."

Stephenson agrees that agricultural ponds can be fantastic big bass fisheries. "They're highly fertile. Fertilizers wash into the pond from the farmer's fields when it rains," he

Lunker Lures For Farm Ponds

A simple, yet well-thought-out, selection of artificials can connect you with a huge farm pond bass. Farm pond experts Chris Stephenson and Greg Bolin provide the following pointers.

■ **Plastic Worm** — "If I had but one lure to fish in a farm pond, this would be it," says biologist and farm pond management consultant Chris Stephenson. "Most fishermen think of worms only for deep water, but they're ideal in shallow ponds, especially when fished around wood cover and undercut banks."

■ **Spinnerbait** — "Especially productive on big fish in ponds where shad have been stocked," Stephenson notes. "In murky ponds, try one with a big, rounded blade and run the lure close to the surface so the water bulges. In cold water, slow roll the lure."

■ **Weedless Lures** — "Often, thick weedbeds in ponds go totally unfished," Stephensen points out. "Work weed holes and edges with a variety of weedless lures."

■ **Buzzbait** — "A big fish lure anywhere you fish it, but especially deadly on farm pond lunkers," Stephenson says. "I caught my biggest pond bass — 9 pounds — on a buzzer."

■ **Topwater Lures** — "The Arbogast Jitterbug has probably caught more 10-pound-plus bass from farm ponds than most other lures put together," Bolin advises. "I've experimented extensively with Jitterbugs, and strongly favor the 5/8-ounce 690 series Weedless Jitterbug in frog/white belly. This lure produces a different sound than other Jitterbugs, which to me is more important than its weedless capabilities. In fact, I'll deliberately make it nonweedless by adding a screw eye with a treble hook to the lure's belly. Fish this at night and hang on!"

SMALL WATERS are often overgrown with grass, making weedless lures like frogs, worms and blade baits top producers.

THE CLASSIC JITTERBUG is legendary for catching trophy bass from farm ponds.

says. "It's been proved time and again that highly fertile ponds are great for lunker bass production."

An avid bass angler, Stephenson recalls a visit to a potential client's pond. "He called me out to have a look at it, telling me that the pond wasn't fished that often. It was really small, about 1 acre. Cows were standing in it — a real mudhole stock pond. Besides that, it was midsummer and the water was at least 90 degrees." Stephenson began his pond evaluation by casting a spinnerbait into the murky water. "On my first cast, I caught a 7-pound largemouth. On my second, I caught a 6. Looking at this pond, you'd never suspect it would hold the quality and quantity of bass that it did."

Some of Stephenson's lunker-producing measures may seem out of sync with today's bass conservation philosophies.

"To grow giant bass, you've got to reduce the number of smaller bass in the pond," he says. "Catch-and-release anglers may cringe at the thought of removing perhaps 300 to 500 10-inch bass from a good-size pond, but if the owner wants big fish, that's exactly what must be done. I recommend reducing the number of smaller fish by at least 20 percent. But once they're gone, you've got to stock those shad to make the plan work. Big bass need plenty of elbow room, and the right kind of forage." Stephenson's best big bass ponds have been thinned to 75 to 100 bass per acre.

It's possible to catch a giant bass from an unmanaged farm pond; your chances escalate dramatically when you pinpoint managed ponds in your search for lunkers.

"One of my ponds had never had a big bass caught from it prior to removing many of the small bass and adding shad," he relates. "After three years of management, the owner caught a 12-pound, 3-ounce giant and two over 10. Another pond we've worked on produces so many 10s, it's unreal. They caught a 14 from it this year."

Stephenson's work with ponds has resulted in observations that can be beneficial to farm pond prowlers.

"Deep water is commonly associated with big bass, but this is more myth than reality, especially in a farm pond," he points out. "Deep ponds are subject to severe stratification. In hot weather, a deep pond may be devoid of oxygen below the 15- to 18-foot zone. Shallow ponds won't stratify, and are often better for producing giant largemouth."

The presence of aquatic grass doesn't necessarily mean the pond will hold big bass. "Too much grass gives the baitfish too many hiding places," he believes. "I prefer as little weed coverage as possible when managing a pond for lunkers."

DOING YOUR HOMEWORK

Gaining access to a farm pond isn't necessarily the first step in fishing it, believes Crossville, Tenn., pond angler Greg Bolin. Knowing which farm ponds hold giant bass requires some digging, he indicates.

"Before I ask the landowner to fish a pond, I try to find out some information about it — how long it's been there, whether or not it's been stocked, and especially if it has a reputation for producing lunkers," he says. "County maps often indicate large numbers of private ponds. There are a great many that you'll never gain access to, but there are enough you'll be able to fish to make the hunt worthwhile."

Bolin has plenty of advice for pond fishermen who hope to gain access to a lunker pond. "First and foremost, keep in mind that this is private property. The landowner doesn't have to let you fish his pond," he advises. "The first step in gaining access is to simply be polite. You've got to try to get to know the landowner before he'll welcome you on his land. Chances are, he's been victimized in the past by people sneaking in, littering, leaving his gates open and so forth. Why should he let you fish? You've got to convince him, and that can only be done face to face."

Once access to the pond has been won, remember that fishing it should be regarded as a rare privilege, Bolin stresses. "Pick the best days to fish it — don't wear out your welcome. Most of my big pond bass have been caught around the full and new moons. I always call ahead to make sure it's all right for me to fish the pond.

"And think of ways you can return the favor. The obvious things are closing gates, packing out your litter and offering to bring the landowner some fish for his table. But it's the not-so-obvious things that can seal your relationship with the pond owner. Find out when his birthday is and send him a card. Help him build a fence or take up hay — it may mean a day of hard work when you could have been fishing, but it may result in years of great fishing."

STALKING TROPHY bass in a float tube is the ultimate farm pond bass fishing experience.

APPROACHES FOR LUNKERS

Greg Bolin prefers to bring in a small boat whenever possible to fish a farm pond.

"Some ponds are just too rough to get a boat into; others, the landowner won't let you use one," he says. "But a boat lets you approach the pond as you might a bigger body of water.

"You can fish ledges offshore, for example. Most anglers associate ledges only with big lakes, but many ponds are full of them. In the area where I live, you can't dig 2 feet into the ground without hitting solid rock, so you can imagine the ledges we find in our local ponds."

In ponds with a rocky bottom, these offshore ledges often outproduce the banks. But in ponds with a mud bottom, fish tend to congregate in the shallows along the shoreline, as well as in lily pads and wood cover, he says.

In a pond with a mud bottom, Bolin tries to make his very first cast count. "You'd be amazed how many giant bass have been caught on an angler's first cast in a farm pond, even by bank fishermen," he says. "I know folks who have caught lunker bass from the pond's bank that hit just as they went to pull the lure from the water, almost right between their legs!

"It pays to use a stealthy approach when walking up to a pond. I try to make my first casts parallel to the bank, not see how far across the pond I can chunk my lure."

Low light periods are prime time for big pond bass, Bolin says. His favorite is the "witching hour" between daylight and darkness.

SEASONAL PATTERNS

Springtime is not the only time
to land a lunker . . .

HOW THE PROS PATTERN TROPHY BASS

Follow these tips from big bass specialists to upgrade the quality of your stringers

THEY ARE KNOWN AS THE SPORT'S big bass magicians, able to conjure heavy fish when others in the tournament field are weighing in average stringers. For example:

• BASS world champion Woo Daves remembers a 15-bass, 96-pound stringer he caught during a two day tournament on Virginia's Kerr Reservoir. Four of the bass weighed over 8 pounds.

• The largest bass that fellow world titleholder Ken Cook ever caught weighed 12 pounds, 11 ounces, and for a time it held the record as the largest bass caught in Lake Sam Rayburn.

• Ron Shuffield's winning stringer in a marquee BASS event held at Lake Okeechobee included bass weighing 9-3 and 6-12. His largest tournament bass ever, weighed 10-4, and he won big bass honors at the 1987 Texas Invitational at Sam Rayburn.

• Mark Davis, a long-time guide on Lake Ouachita and BASS world champion, knows a spot on Ouachita where on a calm day he can catch three or four bass in the 5-pound class. His best day? Ten bass weighing 49 pounds.

Big Bass.

They're on every fisherman's mind, from the time he begins planning his trip to the moment he parks his boat in the garage back home. They're elusive, almost to the point of being mythical, for few anglers ever do catch 5-pound-plus bass on artificial lures with any degree of regularity.

In the tournament ranks, where big bass are more valuable than gold, one would expect the pros to spend all their time trying to pattern the heavyweights, but this is rarely the case. In fact, statistics on big bass success rates question whether it is even possible to establish a pattern for big bass.

But Daves, Cook, Shuffield and Davis think it is.

"First you need to establish what represents a 'big' bass in the lake you're fishing, and whether a reliable population of these fish are present," says Cook, a former fisheries biologist.

"At Sam Rayburn, for example, we know there are lots of big bass in the 4- to 7-pound class there, and that it will take fish of that quality to win a tournament. The same is true at Lake Guntersville in Alabama and at Lake Okeechobee.

"On the other hand, at Lake Mead or on the Ohio River, we know big bass are not common,

so, consequently, we alter our thinking to quantity rather than quality."

"In tournaments, virtually every one of us thinks in terms of catching a limit first," adds Shuffield. "One of the major keys to catching big bass is fishing slower, and when you're fishing for a limit, you're usually fishing fast. Thus, we're working in a contradiction: We want to catch big bass, but we're not using the techniques that would do it."

"Big bass behave a little differently than smaller bass," says Davis. "Smaller fish are a lot easier to catch because they're more aggressive; big bass do not usually chase lures very far."

Big bass also have certain other characteristics and habitat preferences that anglers must recog-

nize if they hope to catch them. Among these are cover, depth, food, current and a preference for big lures.

Here's a snapshot at how Daves, Cook, Shuffield and Davis describe these characteristics:

• *Cover* — "Big bass use what I call 'prime' cover," notes Shuffield. "Smaller fish tend to use the visible cover in shallow water, but big bass are more often found in deeper cover that is completely under water and not visible."

"I believe big bass are more sensitive to fishing pressure," says Davis, "which is why you do find them away from the obvious, heavily fished cover.

"The place I know of on Lake Ouachita where I can catch several big bass is a flat or underwater point near the mouth of a river. The depth

and laydown logs mixed in. I also look for cover near deep water."

• *Depth* — "The first thing to keep in mind about big bass is deep water," says Davis. "You might not actually catch your big bass in deep water, but they'll be near it.

"This can be a ditch, river channel or edge of a point," he continues, "and it doesn't have to be a major drop. Deep water depends on the lake you're fishing. In Lake Ouachita, deep water is 15 to 20 feet and deeper, but on Okeechobee, it might be just 8 or 10 feet."

Says Shuffield, "I catch my larger bass 2 to 5 feet deeper, on average, than the other bass I catch. I really believe this relates to fishing pressure; the big bass retreat to escape the bombardment of lures, trolling motors and boats. We see this quite often in tournaments.

"When I won the Sam Rayburn tournament, I fished the first three days in one area that received very little fishing pressure. On the last day, the spot looked like the ocean, as jet-skiers, pleasure boaters and everybody else crisscrossed it.

"I moved 150 yards away, where the water was about 3 feet deeper, and started catching bass again."

Cook's 12-pound, 11-ounce giant also came from slightly deeper water than where he'd caught fish earlier. "I had five 3-pounders in the boat," he remembers, "which had all come from the back of a flat. I worked out to slightly deeper water, to the very last bush on a point where a creek ran nearby, and that's where I caught it."

• *Food* — "I believe having easy access to food, such as minnows or crawfish, is important to big

WOO DAVES looks for cover near deep water when searching for quality bass.

changes from 10 to 15 feet on top of the flat to 100 feet in the river. There is cover along the edge of that drop, but because it's invisible, people don't fish it."

Davis says he can catch bass there on a calm day, but not on a weekend. Boat traffic over the point pushes the big bass deeper, or at least makes them inactive, he believes.

"Sometimes you can pattern big bass precisely by the cover," says Daves, "but not often. I have seen times when big bass used green willows one day, but the next they were on sweetgums and the following day on something else.

"I prefer two types of cover together when I'm looking for big bass. This can be logs in a field of lily pads, for example, or standing timber with brush bass," says Shuffield. "When I approach an area looking for big bass, I look for bait. If I don't see it, I idle through the area looking at my depthfinder, and if I don't see it there, I don't stop to fish.

"If I do see bait, I look for cover or structure at the depth the bait is located. This can be a channel or grassbed, for instance, and it is best when it produces an edge effect. I always look for bait before I look for bass."

Davis isn't really so sure the presence of baitfish indicates the presence of big bass. Quite often, baitfish schools are surrounded by mediocre bass.

"Big bass don't feed nearly as often as smaller fish," he explains. "I believe big bass always know where the forage is, and when they decide to feed, they know where to go to find it.

"A number of telemetry studies have shown big bass spend much of their time suspended over deep water, but when they decide to feed, they follow a fairly definite route into shallow water. When they finish feeding, they swim back out to deep water and suspend again.

"This is especially true in deep lakes like Ouachita. On shallow lakes with a lot of cover, such as Guntersville, I believe big bass probably do move more. It's possible they also feed more on lakes like this because bait is more widespread."

• *Current* — "In many systems, I think current can be the determining factor in how often a big bass will feed," says Shuffield, whose home water is the Arkansas River.

"In current, big fish seem easier to predict and to catch, because the water flow positions the bass very definitely. They move into the eddy areas and backwaters, where current brings food to them.

Anything that breaks up the current can be a holding place for a big bass."

On big reservoirs, Shuffield continues, wind can have the same effect as current does in a river: It causes baitfish to collect against the windblown shoreline, and the ripples it creates reduce the fish's visibility.

• *Lures* — "Big bass are very efficient predators," says Cook, "which may in part explain their preference for big lures. They don't feed as often, so nature tells them to get the largest meal possible when they do feed.

"Of course," he adds, "all of us have caught big bass on small lures and light lines on occasion, but I firmly believe that day in and day out, larger lures will catch more large bass."

RON SHUFFIELD finds that flowing water positions bass very definitely.

MARCH MADNESS

In warmer sections of the country, March is the time when bass and bass fishermen meet in a frenzy of shallow water action

MARCH MADNESS.

It is a time when the thoughts of men, young and old, turn to college basketball.

It is also a time when serious fishermen know to get ready for the very best their sport has to offer. A magical time is about to occur. For knowledgeable bass anglers, there is no time like their own March Madness.

In fishing terms, March Madness means catching trophy class bass, heavy with eggs and feeding frantically in preparation for the spawn. All across the southern tier of the United States — from the Carolinas to California — March is the month when big schools of prespawn bass provide the fishing of a lifetime.

"As a fisherman, it really gives you a lot of drive," agrees Davy Hite, former BASS world

champion and points race title-holder. "It's prespawn time, and the big females are very predictable. They're on their migration routes to the spawning areas, and you can intercept them in certain predictable places. They group up because they're all headed to the same general spawning areas. And that's when you can catch big fish cast after cast. They're all big, quality female bass."

Adds Oklahoma's Ken Cook, "The prespawn season ends up being the best time of the year to fish because feeding is a prime motivation for the bass at this time. Their metabolism increases as the water temperature increases, and they need to fuel up for the spawn and growth."

"This is the time when you will find schools of monster bass stacked together like no other time of year," adds legendary tournament pro Roland Martin. "There will be 15 or 20 giant bass in one little spot. *Son!*"

Experienced anglers understand that there is nothing quite like the action and anticipation associated with the prespawn period just before this wave of bass heads for the spawning grounds. But like most good things in life, it doesn't last long. The supercharged big bass phase usually begins in the last week of February and extends through the first two weeks or so of March, throughout much of the country.

But it's a blast while it lasts.

To illustrate the kind of slugfest the prespawn stage can provide, Hite recalls his first BASS victory, which occurred in the midst of March Madness on Alabama's Lake Eufaula in 1994. During practice,

the South Carolina pro had pinpointed three stopping points along the bass' major migration routes to large spawning flats. When the tournament concluded, Hite had caught basically all of his winning weight of 67 pounds, 5 ounces from one spot.

Oklahoma pro Jim Morton, a past BASS winner, remembers an early March BASS tournament on Grand Lake in his home state when March Madness was in full force.

"During practice, the fish were so locked into prespawn staging that I could literally pick my place and catch a 5- or 6-pound fish on a Storm ThunderStik (jerkbait)," Morton says. "It was so automatic that I could go down a bank and pick out a little rock jetty or rock point, and I could almost call my shot. It was incredible. On one morning of practice, I caught 25 fish that weighed at least 5 pounds each, by going from place to place with my jerkbait.

"But the first day of the tournament, it was over. It was like somebody had rung a magic bell, and the fish all went to the bank, spread out and started spawning."

March Madness can be a mind-boggling time to be an angler.

In the springtime, the accessible and shallow spawning bass garner the most attention from bass enthusiasts — sometimes to the angler's detriment, according to the experts.

"It's a time of year when a lot of people get caught up in the spawn and go to the bank a little too early," Hite contends. "Sure, they can have fun catching the little male bass that are around the beds on the bank.

"Instead, they ought to be fishing a little deeper and farther offshore. You aren't going to catch as many fish, but when you do find a group of female bass in a staging area, they will be easy to catch, and they will be big ones. That's the kind of place where you're going to win tournaments that time of year."

Enjoy March Madness while it lasts. This special time of year brings with it a degree of predictability that is rare in bass fishing.

The key to locating the earliest of these prespawn marauding bass is to look for the warmest water available in early spring, according to Martin. He notes that the average lake can have a 10 to 15 degree variance in water temperature, depending upon the location of certain coves, shorelines and pockets. During the prespawn period, most of the lake will have a temperature in the 50s, but a few areas will top the 60 degree mark. Those warmer temperature zones will be the earliest magnet areas for prespawn bass.

Nowhere is this predictability better illustrated than in the location that prespawn staging bass utilize each year.

During this time of year, Hite haunts long, sloping points near creek channels, intersecting creeks, and roadbeds in close proximity to creeks. Martin recalls his most memorable prespawn action occurring at the junction of a small ditch with the mouth of a slough that would later serve as spawning grounds in lakes Rayburn, Toledo Bend and Santee Cooper. Morton targets unusual bottom contour features — gravel points and pockets — that extend off the bank.

"The key element for locating prespawn bass are the edges," Cook advises. "Bass tend to follow edges of cover like fencerows, creek channels and roadbeds that serve as pathways for the bass to move from their wintertime areas to the shallows. They move along these edges and stop on breaks in the edge — like corners, intersections in roadbeds, turns in creek channels, and other junction areas."

One of the most attractive aspects of March Madness is that these prespawn females are usually found at accessible depths. In most lakes and reservoirs, 6 to 10 feet seems to be their average depth, depending upon water clarity. In the stained waters that dominate Oklahoma, Morton pinpoints the 4- to 6-foot range as the usual depth of such staging fish.

An important consideration in prespawn location is its proximity to the spawning grounds. Hite has found that these stopping points can be anywhere from 100 to 500 yards from spawning flats and coves. Martin recalls red-hot staging spots that were a half-mile from a massive spawning area.

Regardless of their actual location, these prespawn staging bass are among the most aggressive of the entire year. During March Madness, these bass are even more opportunistic than normal.

"It's just their nature to be superaggressive

Tactics For March Madness

When it comes to catching the aggressive prespawn bass holding on middepth structure or cover, a variety of lures will produce.

Davy Hite's three favorite lures for this miniseason are a large spinnerbait, jig and crankbait. "I alternate all three on each spot," he says. "If I stop catching fish on a crankbait, I'll try slow rolling a spinnerbait. Then I'll slow down with a jig."

Oklahoma pro Jim Morton relies on a suspending version of a jerkbait (Husky Jerk or Storm ThunderStik) and crankbait (Shad Rap or Storm Wiggle Wart).

"My favorite way to catch them is on a suspending jerkbait, but I also catch a bunch on a suspending crankbait like a Wiggle Wart," he explains. "With the crankbait, it depends on the kind of wobble they want on that day. If they want a wide-wobbling crankbait, I'll tie on a Wiggle Wart. If they don't respond to that, I'll go with the Shad Rap, which has a tighter wiggle and provides a more subtle presentation."

Jerkbaits with the brighter color schemes (firetiger, gold, red-and-yellow) seem to produce best during March Madness. But Morton uses crankbaits with a natural crawfish pattern to take advantage of the early spring emergence of crawfish in most lakes.

during this time," Hite explains. "They really feed up before they go in to spawn. The fish seem to know that they have to put on calories for the stressful time ahead."

"I change hooks on almost every lure I throw, but during this time I don't even bother with that," Cook interjects. "They are so aggressive, they really swallow the bait. You don't lose many fish during this period."

Morton emphasizes that the prespawn bass get more active each day as the water temperature rises.

"They will stay in this aggressive mode until either the water warms enough to cause them to move up and start spawning or we have a cold front that lasts two or three days," Morton says.

"The fish will drop back out and suspend in 10 to 12 feet of water if we have a severe cold front. They get in a state of limbo during a severe cold front. And cold fronts are more of a factor in the spring than any other season."

To experience March Madness at its maddest, Roland Martin suggests taking moon phases into consideration. The female bass move onto mid-depth structure in waves with the combination of a full or new moon and water temperatures in the mid-60s. And the absolute best prespawn action usually occurs three or four days before a full or new moon.

"March Madness is a good name for it," Martin says, smiling. "It's without a doubt the best time to be a fisherman."

WHEN SEARCHING FOR big bass, look for unusual bottom contour features that extend off the shoreline.

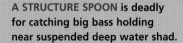

A STRUCTURE SPOON is deadly for catching big bass holding near suspended deep water shad.

WHEN LUNKERS GO TO SCHOOL

In summer or winter, look for big bass to be prowling beneath schools of shad

EN MASSE, SCHOOL BASS are like popcorn — light, lively and a pleasant appetizer. But nobody is satisfied with just one. And nobody wants to fill up on them and forget about the main course — the long-sought trophy largemouth.

The challenge to anglers is that schooling fish and lunkers live in contrasting areas of the lake. In the latter case, the vast space of open water is where the big fish live.

What concentrates offshore fish in catchable numbers? For the little ones, it's baitfish. By midsummer throughout the South and West, threadfin shad have reached the mature 3- to 5-inch size that bass just can't turn down. And gizzard shad, which survive farther north as well as in warmer climes, show about the same growth rate but keep right on growing. The young of the year are still small enough for bass to eat right on into October and November.

Both shad species spend nearly all their time in open water, because that's where the algae and zooplankton they eat are available in greatest abundance, and because the open water is not generally a holding area for predators.

When the baitfish reach a size large enough to make it worth the energy to chase them, young bass from 1 to 3 pounds gather and begin to trail them, like sharks sometimes trail schools of mackerel and tuna in the open sea. When something triggers them, they go on a spree, evidently eating far more than hunger alone calls for — the "feeding frenzy" that turns normally cautious fish into mindless eating machines.

Bass often bite around shad schools even when there's no surface action to tip you off to the location. The characteristic "shad ripple" is the usual indication on calm summer afternoons — it has the appearance of a little cat's paw of wind or busy water on an otherwise calm surface. You can also sometimes home in on cruising shad by watching gulls, which will dip and whirl over the baitfish even when nothing is chasing from below. And shad tend to gather in areas where there is a bit of current, such as in a narrowing of an otherwise broad lake, near bridges spanning causeways, and at the mouths of creeks and bays.

Working shad schools for big fish is not limited to warm weather. The cold-sensitive baitfish head for "temperature refuges" when water temperature drops into the low 60s. They have to, because the chill makes them too sluggish to swim, and most threadfins die if caught in water colder than about 45 degrees. The overwintering adults can be found gathered in large schools wherever the warmest oxygen-laden water in the lake is found.

In power plant lakes, including some as far north as Illinois, the heated outflow is a sure thing to hold shad — and big bass — all winter long. Similarly, spring outflows can create refuges where both oxygen and warmth attract baitfish. And in some lakes, deep water alone can create a blanket layer under which the shad, and the bass, gather.

Top pros are well aware of this winter schooling activity; they keep a sharp eye on their depthfinders for the telltale deep water echoes that indicate a cold weather temperature refuge. And unlike in summer, when fish tend to segregate by size, in winter you may find an 8-pounder swimming shoulder to shoulder with a fleet of 14-inchers.

The depth where the shad gather depends on the water quality. In darkly stained Florida lakes or Louisiana bayous, where little sunlight reaches bottom far from shore and where there's little oxygenating vegetation as a result, the schools may be in water as shallow as 10 or 12 feet. They can't go lower, because there's no oxygen in the deepest water. On the other hand, in clear, rocky lakes of the piedmont

South, there may be oxygen, shad and fish, at depths of 40 feet or more.

In the shallower temperature refuges, the best approach to catching winter bass is to locate the school by making a pass or two over it as you study your depthfinder. After a school is found, back off, anchor and cast sinking offerings, such as a Carolina rigged silver-black worm, to the fish. Sinking plugs, such as the Rat-L-Trap or Countdown Rapala, can also be good at times, though sometimes the fish don't seem to have the energy to chase the faster moving lures in winter.

Spoon jigging is another deadly method for attracting big bass holding close to deep water shad. Experts find fish along the little-known open lake dropoffs, where lime rock ridges form drops of 4 to 6 feet into 12-foot-deep troughs. That's not much of a drop in a mountain country lake, but in the flatlands of southern Florida, it's a major attraction for shad. The pros also score with spoons or heavily weighted plastic worms in the "dynamite holes" dredged out as fill for the berm on the south side of the lake.

The spoon technique employs dense, 1-ounce jigging spoons, such as those made by Hopkins, Mann's and others, which are danced straight up and down over the fish. The spoons may be tied directly to the line or rigged on a 24-inch mono leader, attached to the running line with a barrel swivel to prevent twist.

The lure is allowed to plummet all the way to bottom on free-spool. The angler then puts it into action with an upward flick of the wrist, which makes the spoon dart upward a couple of feet. It's then allowed to flutter back toward bottom as the angler lowers the rod, just fast enough to stay in touch with the fall but not so fast as to create a wave of slack.

The strike usually comes on the fall. Often, the

line simply stops before the lure can reach bottom. Other times, the angler feels just the slightest tick as the fish grabs the spoon. In either case, it takes an instant strike to score, because bass don't hold the hard, metal lure in their mouths long. The exciting part is that when you set the hook, you might slap the barbs into a 12-ouncer that comes shooting to the surface like an overgrown shiner, or you may get your arms stretched by a 12-pounder that's a lifetime trophy. Either way, you can be sure that a good portion of the weight of your catch came from dining on shad.

A BIG JIG FISHED where deep water collides with wood cover can yield huge results.

LURES FOR LUNKERS

You have to think big to catch
a trophy largemouth . . .

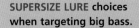

BIG BASS BAITS

If you're hunting a springtime trophy bass, master the use of these lures

L AKE FORK GUIDE and Texas BASS pro Kelly Jordon fondly remembers the autumn day he and a client caught 15 bass while crappie fishing. The 10 largest bass, all caught in a span of half an hour, weighed 101 pounds.

"We were easing along a breakline, steadily catching crappie and a few yellow bass on jigging spoons," he explains. "The fish suddenly stopped biting and disappeared off the depthfinder. It was pretty abrupt, but we stayed where we were, hoping the crappie would come back.

"Instead, what came by was a school of huge bass, and they were hungry. The biggest we landed weighed 11 1/2 pounds, and we lost seven or eight more, including some even larger than that. I'm absolutely convinced the crappie and 'barfish' left because they saw the bass coming."

One spring day in Florida, Melvin Carter, his son, Darryl, and guide David Perkins enjoyed a similarly spectacular day while fishing live golden shiners on Rodman Reservoir. They caught four bass topping 10 pounds, the largest weighing 15-2.

These two examples, while extraordinary, illustrate the fact that trophy bass can be caught on both artificial lures and live bait.

Jigging spoons are not the only lures that produce such results, nor are golden shiners the only live bait that can be used. If your goal this season is to catch a trophy bass, here's a look at some of your best choices.

(Opposite page) JIM MORTON'S 13-pounder fell for a topwater worked around vegetation in clear water.

JIGGING SPOONS

These heavy slabs of lead are fished primarily in the fall and winter, when bass are

FOR BIGGER bass, use bigger worms. Ten- to 16-inchers get the nod from serious trophy hunters.

USE A NOISY prop bait to grab the attention of trophy bass when the fish are schooling.

deeper and the lures can be used to imitate dying shad. As Jordon's example shows, these baits can be extremely effective.

Many anglers actually fish jigging spoons too fast; that is, they lift them off the bottom too far. In winter, when everything moves slowly in the colder water, a spoon only needs to be worked a few inches, which translates into almost minimal rod tip movement.

Spoons are most effective when they fall on a slack line, too. It is still necessary to follow the lure back down by lowering your rod, but you have to do it slightly faster than the lure is sinking. This is what separates the pros from the amateurs in spoon jigging success: Strikes come most often as the spoon is falling on this slack line, but you've got to watch your line to see it happen, since you probably won't feel it.

SPINNERBAITS

Spinnerbaits account for large numbers of trophy bass each year, and they're not relegated to shallow water. Some of today's heavier spinnerbaits (1 ounce or heavier) can be slow rolled right along the bottom to follow an underwater grassline or channel break.

The obvious attractions of spinnerbaits are that they produce vibrations; they're largely weedless, so they can be fished safely around brush; and they're effective throughout the year. The major drawback is that they can't be kept in a specific strike zone very long.

Staying in a small strike zone area isn't really what spinnerbaits are about, anyway. They're designed to bring reaction strikes, and perhaps the best way to do that is with erratic movements during each retrieve.

Each time a spinnerbait falls or begins climbing after a fall, the vibration pattern changes, and strikes most often seem to come immediately after this change occurs. You'll get the most rises and falls with a "yo-yo" retrieve — simply raise your rod tip to make the spinnerbait climb, then lower your rod tip and reel in slack line as the spinnerbait falls. Slowly repeat the process all the way back to the boat. Rhythm is important in this retrieve, so don't hurry the process.

A great retrieve when bass are lurking in water as deep as 30 feet is known as "ripping." Let your spinnerbait fall to the bottom, jerk your rod tip up and reel fast to make the lure jump suddenly off the bottom. You'll need a lure weighing at least 3/4 ounce for this, and it works best when the spinnerbait has a single large Colorado or willowleaf blade.

SWIM BAITS

In California, a category of lures known as "swim baits" has proved to be extremely effective for trophy bass. These lures generally resemble rainbow trout — a favorite food of big bass that is stocked in many state lakes during the fall and winter.

Swim baits fall into two groups: those featuring a full, soft plastic body and rigged with one or more hooks; and those with a hard, molded plastic head and a replaceable soft body, again with one or more hooks. Both are available in sizes ranging from 4 to 12 inches in length, and some are made to float and/or dive, while others are made to sink.

Swim baits can be fished many ways, depending on the type being used. One presentation is simply to cast and reel the lure back slowly and steadily so it looks like a meandering trout. Not surprisingly, this can be extremely effective when the lure is fished around scattered cover in open water. Swim baits are not lures for specific targets, but rather for areas, since they're too large to be cast with any degree of accuracy. Their action comes from the tail designs, which vibrate as the lure is retrieved and which make the bait appear more lifelike.

Another popular technique is "deadsticking," in which the lure is not moved. This can be done with a sinking lure left alone on the bottom, as well as with a floating model. Floating swim baits are often drifted this way along major channel breaks and across wide flats, and big fish come up from surprisingly deep water to hit them.

Swim baits have been used in other parts

Top Lures For Lunkers

Plastic worms continue to be the odds-on favorites of trophy bass, according to reports submitted to the Bassmaster Lunker Club.

Of 626 largemouth entries — all 10 pounds or heavier — accepted over five years, 141 were caught on artificial worms.

The Lunker Club awards certificates and patches to BASS members who catch largemouth weighing at least 10 pounds. Applications request details about lures, retrieves, fishing patterns, weather conditions and other factors involved in the catches.

Live bait accounts for a large percentage (16.7%) of the lunkers, and shiners were the overwhelming choice among live bait anglers. Of 105 bass caught on bait, 95 hit shiners. All but 15 of those shiner-caught bass came from Florida.

Generally, the proportion of big bass caught on various lures reflects those lures' popularity among all fishermen. Jigs and spinnerbaits were second and third in lunker catches, respectively, with 70 and 60 entries. Lizards were used in 54 catches, while crankbaits were tied at 38 with the combined category of soft jerkbaits and floating worms.

Most categories of artificial lures saw the same amount of success, proportionally, compared to an analysis of Lunker Club catches two years before. However, the number of trophy bass caught on plastic lizards nearly doubled, from 19 to 35, and the number of bass caught on soft jerkbaits and floating worms rose from 11 in 1979-1999 to 27 in 2000-2001. A relatively new class of lures, the California-spawned swim baits registered eight trophy largemouth in the past two years. None was caught on swim baits previously.

A total of 39 trophy smallmouth (6 pounds and heavier) were registered with the Lunker Club one year. Jigs were the most effective baits for smallmouth, with 10 catches. Other top offerings include live bait (7), crankbaits (6), jerkbaits (6) and tube lures (5). Smallmouth catches were not included in the charts below.

BASSMASTER LUNKER CLUB SCOREBOARD

Artificial Lures	Catches	Percentage
Plastic Worms	141	27.0
Jigs	70	13.4
Spinnerbaits	60	11.5
Lizards	54	10.4
Crankbaits	38	7.3
Soft Jerkbaits/Floating Worms	38	7.3
Jerkbaits	33	6.3
Topwater Plugs	24	4.6
Lipless Crankbaits	14	2.7
Crawfish/Creature Baits	14	2.7
Buzzbaits	13	2.5
Grubs/Tubes	12	2.3
Swim Baits	8	1.5
Spoons	2	0.4
Total	521	99.9

Live Bait	Catches	Percentage
Shiners	95	90.5
Water dogs	5	4.7
Nightcrawlers	3	2.9
Crawfish	2	1.9
Total	105	100

SWIM BAITS are popular big bass lures in California waters where trout are stocked. A popular trick is "deadsticking" a floating swimmer on the surface.

of the country, with limited success, but only because fishermen elsewhere do not use them nearly as much as they do in California. Some big bass have been caught with them in Lake Fork as well as in Florida lakes.

SOFT PLASTICS

The various types of soft plastic lures, including worms, craw worms, lizards, tubes and the many-legged "creature baits," are among the most effective of all trophy bass lures. Most can be cast accurately to specific targets, and once by a target, the lure's generally large size displaces a lot of water, making it very noticeable.

If there is a rule about using soft plastics for trophy bass, it is to choose a large lure and fish it slowly. To this end, many big bass experts fish plastic worms 10 to 16 inches in length, or lizards at least 8 inches long. Of course, some big fish are caught on 4- and 6-inch plastic worms each year, but not as many as are taken on larger lures. It is accepted that larger bass do not feed as often as smaller fish, and when big ones do go after something, it's usually a larger meal.

Most soft plastic lures, regardless of size, are fished on the bottom.

One major advantage these types of lures have is that all can be rigged totally weedless, cast into the shadowy places big fish live, then kept there. Texas rigging (with or without a pegged sinker) is the most popular way to fish these lures.

Other rigging options include split shotting (even the really big 11- and 12-inch worms are fished with a 1/8-ounce split shot by some big bass experts), Carolina rigging and weightless. A weightless worm (often described as a "floating" worm) can be twitched on the surface or at practically any depth an angler desires.

Carolina rigging, often considered a "numbers" technique, may be used as an exploratory technique in deeper water, where the sinker is used to telegraph information about the bottom. When the sinker slides from soft mud to harder gravel, for example, the sensation is readily apparent to a skilled fisherman. Knowing that bass like hard-bottom areas and that they often hold around such changes in bottom composition, the fisherman can then work that particular spot more efficiently with a different lure.

JIGS

Jigs are favorite lures among many fishermen, and they produce best in lakes filled with shallow, thick vegetation or other cover. They are most efficient when used as target-specific lures pitched or flipped to bushes, logs or holes in vegetation.

Most fishermen adorn their jigs with either a plastic or pork trailer, which slows the lure's fall and also increases its bulk. Most strikes come as the jig is falling after the initial presentation to a target. If nothing happens on that first drop, the lure can be jigged up and down a time or two, but very seldom do big bass pick up a jig being crawled along the bottom.

Few experienced big bass experts use jigs in deep water. The lures are too small, too slow and simply too inefficient compared to jigging spoons, swim baits or even big plastic worms.

TOPWATERS

It would be impossible to calculate the number of 10-pound bass that have been caught with topwater lures, and it's likely that at least as many big bass have been lost on surface plugs as have been boated. The lures are that popular, and they can be that productive, as well.

The rule of using a truly big lure for truly big bass is especially true with topwater baits. Big lures displace more water, they present a greater shadow or outline, and they have bigger hooks. Because topwater fishing normally is best in clear water, most experts believe bass are attracted to these lures both by sound and vision.

It often seems as if the speed of retrieve or the cadence of its motion is more important than the actual lure itself. Normally, slower is better, and sometimes letting the bait sit motionless on the surface is the key. Even the big floating swim baits are frequently fished this way. Many anglers prefer to begin with a slow retrieve and gradually accelerate the retrieve until a strike comes.

While topwater lures can be fished practically anywhere, working them close to shallow cover, or in extremely clear water over deeper well-defined structure, are two of the best situations to use them. Topwater expert and well-known BASS pro and topwater guru Zell Rowland likes to fish his surface lures along the edges of steep breaklines between shallow and deep water, especially where that break is close to the shoreline. Because of their dangling treble hooks, topwater lures do not perform well when cast over grass or other surface vegetation, so the best technique is to work along the deeper outside edges.

JIGGING SPOONS can be extremely effective in winter and fall, since they imitate dying and injured shad.

WHEN BASS are
buried in dense grass,
a popper will draw
them out from their
hiding place.

LUNKERS ON TOP
If surface strikes from 2- or 3-pounders are fun, imagine what a blast from a giant fish is like

A VIOLENT TOPWATER STRIKE is unquestionably one of the supreme thrills in bass fishing. Of course, any bass taken on the surface is fun, but nothing can compare to that magic moment when a "great ol' big 'un" sucks in your topwater offering!

But is catching a lunker bass on top a totally random occurrence, or are there strategies you can employ to increase the size of your surface catch? We recently queried a Tennessee topwater expert on the topic of catching big bass on surface baits. If you've ever dreamed of having a monster bass explode on your Pop-R, Zara Spook or buzzbait, his input can help make it happen.

FINGERNAILS ON A BLACKBOARD

"A noisy topwater lure is like fingernails on a blackboard to a lunker bass," believes Tennessee trophy bass hunter Steve Dodson. "It has the potential of provoking an aggressive and immediate

THESE OVERSIZE topwater baits make major waves on the surface. Big bass hate that.

killing response more than any other lure style."

Dodson, a computer programmer and veteran bass angler, has become adept at catching big bass on a variety of topwater styles in a wide array of venues. "I used to live in Illinois, where I fished small lakes and reclaimed strip mining pits. There, the ultimate thrill was catching a monster bass at night on a Jitterbug. Here in Tennessee, I fish both big reservoirs and small lakes. I've found topwater lures will catch big bass everywhere, as long as you adjust your bait, presentation and tackle to conditions."

Fishing topwaters is a great way to latch on to a huge bass in today's highly pressured fishing environment, Dodson believes. "Today, most local anglers throw spinnerbaits, Carolina rigs and crankbaits; they ignore topwaters. This fact alone makes me want to fish 'em, since quality bass haven't learned to avoid them."

Many anglers who do fish topwaters use them only in late summer and fall, when large numbers of bass school in open water and chase baitfish to the surface. But is this a good time to catch a *big* bass on top? "I've caught very few largemouth over 3 pounds in the jumps," Dodson says. "Almost every largemouth over 5 pounds I've caught on top appeared to be a loner, not part of a school, and was close to cover. I'm not saying you'll *never* see big largemouth schooling on top, but it's rare. Catching bass in the jumps is fun, but if you're like me, you're more interested in hanging one big fish than a boatload of keepers."

Smallmouth bass are a different story, Dodson claims. "I've seen entire schools of huge small-

mouth busting shad on top over rockpiles and on points at Dale Hollow (Tenn.) and Pickwick (Ala.) reservoirs, and it's truly an awesome sight. I once had two big smallies from a school hooked on my Zara Spook at the same time, but was only able to get one in — the other fish tore off the back hook."

Dodson says his biggest topwater largemouth have come from isolated cover.

"Whenever I see that one little brushtop or lone stump 20 feet from any other piece of cover, I'll plunk a topwater lure right on it," he says, "provided the water temperature is 60 degrees or higher."

He adds, "If you cast 10 feet beyond the cover, the bass is on red alert by the time the lure reaches it. That's when you get that tentative swirl or boil on the lure, rather than a solid strike."

A FEW GOOD BAITS

Dodson is particular about which topwater lures he uses in his quest for big bass. He listed the following as his proven lunker catchers:

TROPHY ANGLER Steve Dodson divides topwaters into six categories, and he believes each type has a specific application.

STEVE DODSON finds topwaters are productive when the water temperature is above 60 degrees.

Stickbait — "The Heddon Zara Spook is the gold standard in this category. It's particularly effective on main lake structures like points and humps in deep, clear reservoirs, and is the best surface lure for trophy smallmouth. It's not a particularly noisy bait, but it's extremely erratic when retrieved in the classic walk-the-dog manner — this probably simulates a fleeing baitfish to bass. Big smallmouth will swim up 20 feet to plaster a yellow Spook."

Buzzbait — "This is a good choice around shallow wood and thin grass cover, if the conditions are right. I catch my biggest fish on buzzers in choppy water, where most bassers don't even use topwater baits. In calm water, usually thought of as buzzbait water, I catch smaller bass on it. Either white or black will work, and I use a trailer hook. I don't stay with a buzzbait long; if I don't get bit on it pretty quickly, I'll switch to another topwater style."

Prop bait — "This is one of the noisiest surface styles; it needs to be used judiciously, or it'll spook 'em. I like it on stormy days or when the water is murky. This is a lure you should definitely cast right to isolated cover instead of beyond it; it's the ultimate reaction-strike bait. A buddy of mine recently caught an 11 3/4-pound largemouth on a blue Gilmore Jumper."

Floating minnow — "A good topwater choice in postspawn, when big bass are hanging around shallow cover and not particularly aggressive. Just cast it around flooded bushes, twitch it once and let it sit — they'll suck it in. It also works on unseasonably mild days in prespawn; I've caught big largemouth and smallmouth on minnow baits in 52 degree water. My favorite is the A.C. Shiner No. 450, bone with orange belly."

Jitterbug — "An awesome night surface lure. Cast it parallel to the shoreline or weed edges in farm ponds, strip pits or small natural lakes, and reel slowly and steadily. I like the magnum-size Musky Jitterbug in black or frog; we used to wear out big bass on it at night in those Illinois strip pits. And if you think *this* is a big bait, there's a guy in south Georgia who hand-carves an outrageous version of a Jitterbug that's almost as big as a loaf of Wonder Bread; he's caught 16-pounders on it at night!"

Popper — "A good bet when largemouth are in milfoil or hydrilla that doesn't quite reach the surface. The Rebel Pop-R isn't a big lure, but it'll catch big fish. I also like the Viva Bug I popper — it's not as loud as Pop-Rs, but it spits up a storm. Of course, the all-time lunker champ in this category has to be the Arbogast Hula Popper. When was the last time you threw one?"

Scum frog — "The only realistic choice for fishing pond scum, lily pads and other high coverage vegetation. Just crawl it across the slop, then when a fish blows up on it, wait 'til you feel it pull before setting the hook. You'll catch bigger bass by probing way back into the thickest cover instead of taking the easy route and fishing the outside edges."

Dodson's favorite topwater rods are stiff 6-foot baitcasters retrofitted with pistol grips, a handle style he finds far more conducive to working these lures than the long handles currently in vogue. For smallmouth in clear reservoirs, he uses 14-pound Excel monofilament, but spools up with 30-pound Silver Thread when fishing prop baits, slop frogs and Jitterbugs around heavy cover for lunker largemouth. "Thirty-pound Silver Thread is the same diameter as many 15-pound monos," he points out. "It's superlimp and exceptionally abrasion resistant, something to consider when gunning for big bass in brushy cover." He'll fish lighter topwater styles (Pop-Rs, A. C. Shiners) on a 6-foot spinning worm rod with 12-pound Excel.

More Topwater Insights

Big bass hunter Steve Dodson shares more insights gleaned from three decades of successful big bass topwater fishing:

■ Although most of his big topwater largemouth were caught in shallow water, they usually were close to deeper water, such as a creek channel or ditch, when they struck. The Tennessee basser feels these superior fish may spend much of their time in the deeper areas, sliding up into the shallows only when hunting for food.

■ While most bassers think sunrise and sunset are prime topwater time, Dodson has caught some of his biggest bass on surface lures in the middle of the day. This includes both smallmouth chasing shad schools in open water, and largemouth parked on isolated cover. Bass associated with cover usually hold in the shade once the sun gets high.

■ Big topwater lures catch bigger bass — some of Dodson's biggest largemouth were taken on the giant Musky Jitterbug. Lunker bass often feed infrequently and want a full-meal deal when they do feed. You can also fish bigger lures on heavier tackle and line, thereby increasing your odds of landing big fish.

■ Small waters — farm ponds, strip pits, private lakes — are a great place to refine your topwater skills for lunker bass. These venues often have plenty of big fish in them, making it easier for you to determine which lures and presentations trigger strikes from quality bass.

ADDING A trailer hook to a buzzbait will increase the odds of a solid hook set.

BIG BASS have bigger appetites, making larger lures a key to landing lunkers.

RUN HEAVY, RUN DEEP: SPINNERBAITS FOR BIG BASS

Whether you're after big smallmouth or heavy largemouth, an overweight spinnerbait can turn the trick

I F WORD SPREAD about big bass being caught on spinnerbaits from a local lake, nearly every angler who heard about it would be hurling 3/8-ounce spinnerbaits around shallow cover that next weekend. After all, isn't that where big bass are caught on spinnerbaits?

Not when Roger Stegall is doing the casting. In fact, if that rumor circulated around Pickwick Lake or the Tennessee-Tombigbee Waterway, it's quite possible that Stegall would be the source of those big fish rumors.

Stegall is a big bass expert who loves feeding spinnerbaits to structure-relating bass. But not just any spinnerbait. He likes them heavy so he can hurl them into the teeth of a ferocious wind and bounce them along the bottom in places that most people don't consider to be "spinnerbait water."

His favorite lure is a modified 3/4-ounce Strike King Premier Model. The standard Premier is dressed with a small Colorado blade and a No. 5 willowleaf, but Stegall removes the Colorado blade, clevis and beads so that only the willow dangles above the hook.

"The Colorado hampers me in deep water because it gives the bait too much lift," he explains. "Also, when I let the bait flutter, the Colorado cuts the flow of water around the willowleaf blade and kills the feel of the lure. By removing it, I can move the bait faster and still keep it down."

Stegall's presentation is a form of slow rolling. He casts beyond the primary target and engages the reel promptly to make the spinnerbait fall on a tight line. He says some strikes occur as the lure flutters over the structure, so he wants to be ready.

Once the spinnerbait hits bottom, he lifts the rod slightly to get the blade turning, then slowly cranks the reel handle about 10 turns to move the lure along the bottom.

"I want to keep the spinnerbait within a foot or two from the bottom," he describes. "After 10 cranks, I stop and let it fall, and that often creates a strike. If not, I make 10 more turns and stop it again, repeating the process throughout the retrieve. It's similar to pumping a worm or jig down a ledge."

(Opposite page) TWO PLUSES of a heavy spinnerbait: It can be cast into the wind and worked deep.

BIG BLADE experts let the bait fall on a tight line before beginning the retrieve.

SOMETIMES BASS will not fall for fakes. In such cases, live bait is the only way to go.

FISH 'CRITTERS' FOR BIG BASS

Sometimes the oldest and wariest bass will fall only for live bait

THE MARK OF a tournament angler is his prowess at catching bass on artificial lures. Still, many recreational anglers rely on natural baits to enhance their chances of catching fish, and for good reason — bass are temperamental creatures, frequently reluctant to attack anything that isn't alive.

Veteran big bass guides often have to resort to using "critters" under tough conditions to generate at least minimal action, particularly when guiding novices on our small, heavily pressured waters.

Fishing with live bait, however, does not automatically guarantee success. Even with natural offerings, it is important to know precisely which live bait to use, how to rig it and the best ways to fish it under various fishing conditions. Following are some of the basic techniques anglers can utilize to catch fish on live baits.

NIGHTCRAWLERS

These magnum worms remain one of the most popular entrees on the live bait menu. Most nightcrawlers are sold by commercial bait vendors. It is important to be rather selective when purchasing a container of these worms — get the liveliest, largest worms you can.

The experts' preferred method for fishing nightcrawlers is to rig them weedless using a No. 6 to No. 8 long-shank bronze bait-holder hook. These hooks are distinctively small, compared to the specialized hooks Bassmasters use for rigging plastic worms.

Tie this hook onto 6- to 10-pound monofilament; the lighter line will let the 'crawler move with minimal restriction. Next, carefully hook the worm through the prominent "sex band" located at the upper third of the body behind the head portion of the bait. Then — and here's the trick — embed the point of the hook back into the thick collar to make the bait practically weedless. This also allows the worm to slither and twist seductively, as it does in its natural state.

(Opposite page) TROPHY EXPERTS use the biggest shiners they can find since trophy bass need bigger servings to fill their bellies.

In many situations, such as fishing heavy brush, rocks and riprap, thick mossbeds and clear water, you will want to make a gentle lob-cast while using the 'crawler without any sinker. The bait will slowly sink to the bottom. Expect most hits on the fall.

If you are working a nightcrawler in deeper water or in windy conditions, it may be necessary to add some weight.

LIVE CRAWFISH can be irresistible to big bass. Fish them in the same areas where you'd throw a fake one.

ALTHOUGH PRETTY **difficult to keep alive, shad can be deadly on big bass, making the outcome well worth the effort.**

Small, BB-size lead shot crimped about 12 to 18 inches above the hook works fine. Or, before you tie on the bait-holder hook, run your line through a little 1/16- to 1/8-ounce bullet sinker. Then carefully crimp the nose of the weight so it stays 12 to 18 inches above the worm.

Regardless of how you present the nightcrawler, always try to keep it moving to some degree. By "inching" the worm along with a slow, intermittent retrieve, you will not only cover more territory, but will also ensure that the bait hasn't become lodged behind a rock or hidden inside a weedbed.

CRAWFISH

Some of the largest bass tallied each season from coast to coast are caught on live crawfish. Crawfish comprise a major source of forage on most inland waters. All the bass species readily attack these small crustaceans.

In some areas, adept anglers may catch their own crawfish using baited traps or nets. In other locales, crawfish are sold in specialized bait shops.

The most effective hook for crawfish is a long-shank, bronze bait-holder hook in No. 1 to No. 6 sizes, depending on the size of the bait. You can scale up in line diameter when working crawfish to anywhere from 8- to 15-pound-test mono. Run the hook through the bony structure between the crawfish's eyes (but not through the brain). This permits the crawfish to move its tail freely as it swims and crawls.

These baits perform best with minimal weight. Use a sinker only if wind or depth makes it necessary. It also helps to slowly retrieve the crawfish (pausing for longer periods than with the nightcrawler) to keep it from hiding in obstructions.

Work the crawfish by slowly "stitching" the bait in, pulling your line by hand, gathering slack after every few feet.

Mike Folkestad of Yorba Linda, Calif., is con-

sidered a big fish expert out West with over 50 bass topping 8 pounds to his credit. The crawfish is among his favorite types of bait.

"I still like to fish with bait once in a while when I'm looking for a big fish, and it won't eat artificials," says Folkestad. "As you soak crawfish on the bottom, watch for telltale signs that a bass is contemplating attacking the bait. Fish the 'dad on a small amount of slack line. If the bait gets excited when a hungry bass is in the vicinity, it may swim frantically, which is signaled by quick twitches in the line. Stay alert!

"When a bass decides to eat the crawfish, usually you will feel a prominent 'thump' on the line as the fish moves to crush the bait. Then, the bass will turn, starting its run. Pick up the slack, follow the fish for a few seconds with the rod tip, then swing hard."

SHINERS

Bassmasters in the South and West will attest to the effectiveness of shiner minnows as great bait for big bass. In less populated areas, anglers often catch their own shiners on small, gold trout hooks baited with bread dough or meal worms. Some bait vendors also stock these minnows, which require special aerated tanks to keep them alive.

Shiners may also be sorted into small, medium and large sizes. The rule, "big baits equal big bass," definitely holds true for shiner fishing. Dedicated trophy hunters looking for big Florida-strain bass in San Diego's small impoundments, for example, try to buy the biggest shiners available.

The most common way to fish these minnows is to suspend them underneath a bobber. The float will serve to keep the shiner from swimming too far back into the tules or other weeds near the bank.

Another strategy is to "fly-line" the bait, without any weight. The minnow will feel very little resistance as it swims freely.

One of the simplest ways to rig a shiner is to run a long-shank bait-holder hook through the minnow's upper and lower lips. By sealing the minnow's lips in this manner, you can minimize the chances of accidentally drowning the baitfish by forcing too much

Making Critters Weedless

Quite frequently one of the problems the live bait fisherman faces when using an open hook point is getting snagged on brush, rock and similar obstructions. You can quickly remedy this by making your live bait hooks weedless.

After threading a shiner, crawfish, or shad on the hook, embed a tiny piece of plastic worm on the point of the hook, making sure to cover up the barb. Try to match the chunk of soft plastic to the color of the natural bait for maximum camouflage.

The soft plastic cap will now make the live-bait hook remarkably weedless, without impeding the movement of the critter. When you set the hook, the point will easily pass through the soft plastic and penetrate the fish's tissue.

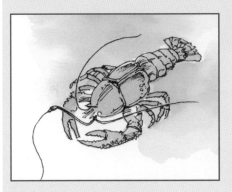

MATCH CRAWFISH to the size and color of the forage in the lake you're fishing.

LIVE SHINERS can be fished on a small-bait hook. For deep bass, weight the line 18 inches above the bait.

WATER DOGS can save the day at times when nothing else attracts the attention of bass.

water through its gills. Hook size may vary from a No. 4 to 2/0, depending on the size of the shiner.

If you cast shiners in heavy cover or over rocky terrain, consider switching to a short-shank live bait hook in sizes No. 4 to 4/0. This style hook, normally used in saltwater circles, will get hung up less often than a long-shank hook.

As with nightcrawlers and crawfish, it is important to give the bass plenty of time to eat the shiner. Quite frequently, the fish will make an initial pass at the minnow, but without really taking the bait. In this situation, try reeling the shiner in a few feet. Often the bass senses that its prey is scurrying away, so it quickly moves in for the kill. A sustained run with the shiner should follow the second attack.

Shiners should also be kept in either your boat's livewell or in a separate aerated bait box. An aquarium dip net is useful for retrieving the minnows from the tank.

SHAD MINNOWS

Along with crawfish, shad comprise the other major forage in many impoundments. Although somewhat fragile, shad are also a potent option for the serious bait fisherman.

Shad can be caught by dropping cast nets onto schools of baitfish as they concentrate near the surface, or they can be caught or snagged by dropping shiny spoons after deep schools of baitfish have been metered.

Like shiners, shad must be kept in an aerated environment and handled gingerly. They should be hooked either through both lips, or through the back, behind the dorsal fin. A thin-wire Sealy hook in No. 1 to No. 6 sizes will work best with the smaller baits, doing minimal damage to the minnow. Switch to stronger forged bait hooks with palm-size shad, or when using these minnows in thick cover.

Shad can be fished shallow or deep. At times, they can be red hot when "fly-lined" weightless in shallow brush, where finicky bass are rooted in tight.

For the deep water approach, crimp on a small lead shot and fish shad all the way down to 60 feet. Allow the bass to run off 1 to 2 feet of line before setting the hook. You can get by with 6- to 10-pound mono when split shotting shad deep, and you need to treat the bait gingerly, since hooks will pull out easily from this bait.

TROPHY BASS TACTICS

You need a game plan to zero in on a big bass . . .

HAIR JIGS are perfect shad imitators, especially when the baitfish are clinging to deep structure.

GAME PLAN FOR DOUBLE-DIGIT BASS

Want to catch a 10-pounder? Who doesn't?
Here's a game plan to make that dream a reality

ONE AFTERNOON IN a place called Birch Creek on Lake Fork, Texas, guide Richard McCarty and two clients were happily casting spinnerbaits to a school of bass ranging between 2 and 4 pounds. It was easy fishing, letting the big willowleaf baits fall, then slow rolling them just above the bottom and waiting for the strike.

McCarty had just reeled in a 4 1/2-pounder and made another cast when he felt a heavier-than-usual strike. When he reeled that fish in, it went straight to the scales; there it registered an even 11 pounds.

"That fish serves as a perfect example of what trophy bass fishing is all about," says McCarty, who has caught more than 40 Lake Fork bass topping 10 pounds. "On a lake known for big bass, a 10-pounder can come at any time, and a fisherman simply has to be ready when that time happens."

With lakes like Fork and Rayburn in Texas, Toho in Florida and Castaic in California regularly producing bass weighing 10 pounds or more, the opportunity to catch a giant has probably never been better. At the same time, however, the rules for catching these bass have not really changed over the years. It still takes time and skill, the proper equipment and timing, and probably a little luck.

"The first thing a serious fisherman must do is identify a true trophy bass lake that has a viable population of bass weighing 10 pounds or more," explains McCarty. "Lake Fork certainly qualifies in that respect, as its record shows, but there are other trophy lakes across the country.

"State game and fish departments can provide a list of the best trophy lakes in their states, but an angler should study the list carefully. If a lake has a viable population of big bass, those fish will show up in creel surveys over a continuous period of time, not just as scattered individual fish.

"In other words, a fisherman looking for a 10-pounder should plan to fish a lake that has a history of producing 10-pounders."

What is most interesting to note about trophy bass lakes in general is that while a

(Opposite page) YOU WILL very rarely catch a truly big bass by accident. Before launching your boat, have a solid plan intact for attacking the trophies in the water you are fishing.

TIMING CAN be crucial to big bass hunters. The spring spawn is the most consistent time frame for wrangling a bruiser female.

10-pounder can come from virtually any part of a lake, historically every trophy fishery has areas that produce big fish consistently. This is true in Fork's Birch Creek, Rayburn's Black Forest, Santee Cooper's Hatchery, the Monkey Box at Okeechobee and numerous other hot spots. Before investing the time and effort for a 10-pounder, a fisherman should be aware that such areas do exist. A little advance research can shorten his trophy hunt.

"One of the things trophy bass fishing requires is more thorough fishing of specific areas," McCarty explains, "and this is one of the main advantages of hiring a guide. You may not be able to see cover on the bottom or understand how a creek channel turns, but a good guide will know what's down there, and he'll be able to tell you exactly how and where to cast."

Having a qualified guide who understands the habits of big bass and who fishes a lake practically every day is also important in creating a level of confidence. With few exceptions, the lakes that support a coterie of full-time bass guides are consistent trophy producers.

"If you don't know a guide on the lake you want to fish," advises McCarty, "make inquiries at different marinas or at the nearest Chamber of Commerce. Sooner or later, one or two names will begin surfacing more than others. On the average, a good guide will charge between $150 and $250 per day, depending on the lake."

In more than a decade of guiding on Lake Fork, McCarty has distilled pure trophy bass fishing into five major categories. These include time of year, tackle and lure selection, water depth, available food and mental attitude. When an angler puts all five of these together, he will be successful most of the time.

TIMING

"Throughout most of the South, the prime time to catch a big bass is in February and March," explains McCarty. "This is the spring spawn, and the big bass are accessible in shallow water. This is also when female bass will be the heaviest.

"Of course, if you're on a trophy bass lake, any bite you get any time of year has the potential to be a big fish. The largest bass I've ever caught, a 14-1, came in December. Overall, however, if you schedule a trophy fishing trip in early spring or perhaps in September and October, when fish are moving shallow to feed, your chances will be better."

Timing is also important for the days of the month as well as the hours of the day. If you can be on the water fishing on those days when the moon rises or sets at the

Notes On Lunkers

These statistics from Bassmaster Lunker Club application forms should help you know when, where and how to catch a wallhanger.

■ Artificial baits rule in big bass territory outside Florida. Soft plastics accounted for 38.9 percent of all lunkers caught; artificial worms (included in that total) hooked 23.7 of big bass.

■ In the hard bait category, jig-and-pigs, spinnerbaits and crankbaits caught almost equal numbers of big bass. Together, they resulted in 30 percent of big bass.

■ Almost all of the 10-pound-plus bass registered came from the Sunbelt. Transplanted Florida-strain bass have flourished in warm locales (with long growing seasons) outside their home range. Leading the lunker race: Florida, Texas, California, Arizona, Georgia and Louisiana.

■ Weather seemed to have little effect; about half the lunkers were caught in clear weather, and the rest, under cloudy or rainy skies.

■ No big fish were caught in water colder than 44 degrees. The largest proportion (38.5 percent) hit in water between 60 and 70 degrees.

Statistics regarding catches during certain moon phases and solar-lunar activity periods were inconclusive. However, trophy hunter Jeffrey Smith believes both factors have much to do with his success. He schedules vacation trips to Florida exclusively for the periods of three days before and after a full moon or a dark moon.

"The dark and full moons are about equal in performance," he says, "and I've never caught a bass over 10 pounds when fishing outside one of those two key moon phases."

He's a firm believer in the effectiveness of charts showing major and minor feeding times. "Especially when I'm fishing in my home area," Smith says, "I live and die by *Bassmaster*'s 'Astro Tables.' They work for me 70 to 80 percent of the time."

Time Of Year Lunkers Were Caught

Month	Percentage Of Catches
January	13.2
February	13.2
March	20.2
April	17.3
May	8.8
June	7.4
July	4.4
August	4.8
September	3.3
October	2.6
November	2.2
December	2.6

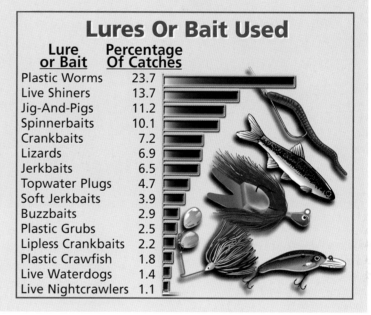

Lures Or Bait Used

Lure or Bait	Percentage Of Catches
Plastic Worms	23.7
Live Shiners	13.7
Jig-And-Pigs	11.2
Spinnerbaits	10.1
Crankbaits	7.2
Lizards	6.9
Jerkbaits	6.5
Topwater Plugs	4.7
Soft Jerkbaits	3.9
Buzzbaits	2.9
Plastic Grubs	2.5
Lipless Crankbaits	2.2
Plastic Crawfish	1.8
Live Waterdogs	1.4
Live Nightcrawlers	1.1

same time the sun is up, you'll generally find big bass more active. This has been proved time and again, not only by guides, but also by tournament pros, whose style of fishing seldom lends itself to catching trophy bass. On other days, McCarty has noted the majority of his big bass come between the hours of 11 a.m. and 2 p.m.

TACKLE AND LURES

"The most common mistake I see clients making is not having the proper equipment for big fish," emphasizes the Lake Fork guide. "I advise them to use 25- to 30-pound-test line on stout, heavy-action rods and reels. With line this strong, you simply do not have to worry about breaking it. You'll have plenty of other problems to think about as it is.

"Stories about catching 10-pound largemouth on light tackle are common, but stories about losing 10-pound bass on light tackle are far more numerous. Most big bass

A BIG 'ol slow rolled spinnerbait will consistently dupe lunkers holding near channel ledges and deep cover.

are caught in or very close to extremely heavy cover — often cover you never see — and I like the freedom to pitch my lure into that cover without thinking twice about whether I can bring a fish out of it."

As a general rule, big bass prefer big lures, too. Baits like 1-ounce bucktail jigs, 10-inch plastic worms, 3/4-ounce willowleaf spinnerbaits and big topwaters like Zara Spooks take far more trophy largemouth than 4-inch finesse worms and 1/4-ounce spinnerbaits.

"Big bass are not as active as smaller fish, and they seem to prefer one-bite/one-meal opportunities," says McCarty. "Every big bass I've ever caught, including a lot between 8 and 10 pounds, has come on a large lure. I'll use a 1/2-ounce spinnerbait a lot, but I always dress it up with a pork or plastic trailer to make it seem larger.

"Using big lures goes right along with using heavier tackle. You need heavier gear to cast and work these larger lures properly. If a client books me specifically for trophy fishing, I always tell him to bring big lures; if he doesn't have any, we'll use mine."

WATER DEPTH

One of the characteristics McCarty and other big bass guides have noticed is that larger trophy fish are nearly always 2 to 5 feet deeper than smaller fish, except during the spring spawning season. If he's consistently catching 2- to 3-pounders, McCarty works his way into deeper water for larger bass.

"Big bass are not always in really deep water, by any means," he explains, "but they're usually very close to it. Ditches, channels and the ends and edges of points all attract and hold big bass. I think one of the reasons Birch Creek produces big bass so consistently on Lake Fork is because the creek is big and very well-defined; there is a distinct break between the flats on the edge of the creek and the creek channel itself.

"The more cover available along the edge of a channel, the better it will produce," adds McCarty, "but isolated cover is important, too. A big bass will dominate a single piece of cover like a stump or clump of vegetation, so they need to be fished as well."

FOOD

McCarty likes to see creeks and coves teeming with baitfish, because he knows it improves his chances for connecting with a big bass. When he does see shad, his immediate reaction is to tie on a spinnerbait with a blade as large as Size 7 and slow roll it around the best cover in the area.

"Easy access to food is important to trophy bass, because they simply do not swim as far as smaller bass do to chase down bait," he explains. "I think this is another reason big bass spend so much of their time in heavy cover. It provides a better hiding opportunity for them when they're waiting for bait to move past.

"What you begin to see when you start putting everything together," he says, "is that it's all inter-related. Baitfish, cover, slightly deeper water equals big bass. None of us completely understands that formula, but it exists. Very, very rarely do you ever catch big bass out by themselves and away from food, cover or deeper water."

MENTAL ATTITUDE

McCarty believes an angler's mental attitude is one of the true keys to hooking and landing a 10-pounder on any lake. He often compares pursuing trophy bass to trophy deer hunting, which he also does each fall.

"Purely and simply, you have to be mentally prepared," he says. "You don't get many chances for bass weighing 10 pounds or more. You have to concentrate, and you may have to do it for several days. One of the prerequisites for trophy bass fishing is giving yourself time. Many of my trophy bass clients book me for three straight days, which is what most guides recommend."

Mental preparedness also comes into play when you finally do hook that trophy.

"Once you do hook a big fish, you can't be tentative playing it," he emphasizes. "You have to take charge instantly and continue to move and control the fish. Once you think about the possibility of losing the fish, the potential for losing it increases dramatically." That's another reason it's so important to have strong equipment.

"You have to always, always expect a big bass, and treat every cast as if it's going to happen that time," McCarty stresses, "because you don't know when it is going to happen. It takes a lot of concentration, which is difficult for many casual anglers. Every bass guide, myself included, can tell you horror stories about giant fish a client let escape for one reason or another."

When he's trying to catch a 10-plus, McCarty fishes more thoroughly — but not necessarily slower — than usual.

He still tries to present his lure to as many fish as possible, but he fishes it more carefully. He raises his jig slowly off the bottom and stops if he feels any pressure at all. He lets his spinnerbait bump every stick and stump. And he casts to every nook and cranny he can spot.

"This is probably the hardest thing for my clients to understand about trophy bass fishing: You simply have to be thinking 'big bass' all the time. When I caught that 11-pounder on the spinnerbait in Birch Creek, we stayed there another hour and a half and caught at least 30 more bass, but none of them topped 4 pounds.

"That's just the way it happens."

Weighs And Means For Lunkers

If you've caught a 10-pounder — or you think you might — remember these tips for documenting your catch.

■ **Always carry a camera** — Disposable cameras are small and inexpensive. Pack one in a watertight plastic bag and keep it with your tackle.
■ **Measure the length and girth** — Lay the fish on a wet, flat surface and measure from the tip of the lower lip to the tip of the tail for the length. To obtain the girth, wrap a flexible tape measure (or string) around the fish at its widest point.
■ **Keep scales handy** — Both digital and spring scales are affordable and fairly accurate. To check the accuracy of your scales, weigh a container filled with exactly one gallon of water. Weigh the same container empty and subtract the weight of the container. The water should weigh 8.3125 pounds.
■ **Release your catch** — Unless your bass is heavier than 22 pounds, 4 ounces, return it to the water after photographing, weighing and measuring. If it does beat 22-4, keep it alive.

SAVVY TROPHY hunters know that quality fish live in numbers lakes.

CATCH BIGGER BASS FROM 'NUMBERS' LAKES

Just because your home lake is loaded with short bass doesn't mean you can't find a few lunkers

DURING A BASS CLUB tournament several years ago, two anglers encountered a giant school of largemouth bunched up on a chunk-rock bank in the back of a tributary arm. For an hour and a half, nearly every cast with a 1/4-ounce crankbait resulted in a strike.

Incredible fishing, to be sure, but even more incredible was the sad fact that neither of them finished in the money. Together, they boated over a hundred bass, but the two fishermen weighed in only two keepers that barely squeaked past the 12-inch size limit. Out of 21 teams competing, the pair that won the pot had but five keepers that tipped the scales at a scant 6 pounds, 2 ounces.

The tournament fishery and the above scenario was a good example of a "numbers" lake — a body of water that produces large, sometimes massive, quantities of small bass, but relatively few quality fish. Numbers lakes can be found nationwide; there may be one near you.

Some bass fishermen will argue that it's fun to catch any bass, even a little one. If you're like most anglers, however, you'd rather get one solid strike from a good fish than catch a dozen shorties. Trouble is, on some lakes there are so many small bass, the quest for a decent-size fish, let alone a lunker, can get mighty frustrating.

How can you separate the wheat from the chaff on a numbers lake? Is it possible to catch numbers of good-size bass — even an occasional lunker — from waters with a reputation of giving up only small fish? These questions were posed to an expert, Guy Eaker, whose pro tournament career spans three decades. His suggestions will have you pulling quality fish from waters where you and your fishing buddies have taken only dinks before.

(Opposite page) COMMON LOGIC says to downsize lure choices on numbers lakes. In doing so, you eliminate your chances of catching a big bass, says Guy Eaker.

TO SEPARATE the men from the boys, upsize. Small fish won't readily eat big baits — big bass will.

A ZILLION A DAY

"Numbers lakes are absolutely loaded with small bass," says Eaker. "On some you can catch a zillion a day, and hardly any will measure. On

CREEK ARMS with flowing water have highly oxygenated water — and bigger bass.

others, you may have to fish through 20 or 30 dinks before you catch a keeper."

Lake Norman, near Eaker's home, is chock-full of undersized bass, the pro noted. "It's not out of the question to catch a hundred small fish a day here. I've fished lakes in Michigan where you'd catch 50 smallmouth in an afternoon, none of which would keep. Numbers lakes are everywhere, and they can be a real challenge."

Occasionally a BASS tournament will be held on a numbers venue. "Cordell Hull Reservoir (Tenn.) and the Ohio River come to mind as tournament locations that were full of small bass," Eaker recalls. "Getting a paycheck in a numbers lake demands strategies that somehow tip the odds of catching larger fish in your favor — and this can take every bit of skill an angler can muster."

Why are some bass waters so top-heavy with small fish? Eaker provided some answers:

• *Short growing season* — Numbers lakes are especially common in the upper Midwest and Northeast, where cold water and a short growing season keep the average size of the bass small.

• *Improper management* — Some management practices, especially high length limits, can put lakes out of balance. If you have to throw back everything under, say, 15 inches, the lake can have a disproportionate number of small bass. The fewer bass in the lake, the greater their potential for growing big.

• *Intense pressure* — On a highly pressured body of water, it's possible that most of the quality bass have already been caught. If these superior fish are kept, they're permanently removed from the gene pool; over time, this can result in a stunted bass population. If they're released, they learn from the experience and may not bite so readily in the future. You can see this phenomenon at work in California's famed lunker lakes, where the big bass have been caught and released so many times, they've become extremely cautious about biting.

TAPPING IN

When trip after trip to a lake yields nothing but scores of bank-runner bass, catching a lunker from the same body of water seems nearly impossible. But Eaker has a reputation for plucking diamonds from such coal mines. In spite of the fact that Lake Norman, Eaker's home lake, has a giant population of small bass, the pro has caught largemouth as big as 9 pounds, 4 ounces there.

"You can tap into the bigger fish if you analyze the situation and pay strict attention to where and how you fish," he promises. If your local waters have yielded mostly dink bass, read what follows carefully — it can put you on the path to better fish.

"Fishermen who frequent a numbers lake often downsize their lures," Eaker has found. "They figure that since they're catching so many small fish, they might as well use small baits and lighter tackle.

"Admittedly, there's some logic to this; it's a lot more fun to catch a 10-inch bass on a light spinning outfit than heavy baitcasting gear, and you'll catch more of them on small baits than big ones. But what these anglers don't realize is that by downsizing their lures, they're often guaranteeing that bigger fish won't bite. It becomes a self-fulfilling prophecy: You're only catching small bass, so you switch to small baits, which in turn guarantees that you'll keep catching small bass."

Eaker makes a point of using big lures in numbers lakes. Long worms, bulky jigs and large spinnerbaits will garner a lot more attention from a quality bass than smaller artificials.

IT'S TIME to upgrade to bigger baits and change locations if the bass coming into the boat are small.

"If I'm catching lots of dinks on a 6-inch worm, I'll switch to a 10-inch ribbon tail worm," he says. "If I'm not getting quality bites on a 1/4-ounce spinnerbait, I'll switch to a 3/8- or 9/16-ounce lure, and increase the blade size to produce greater flash and vibration. Instead of using a 3-inch grub in a superclear lake, I'll use a 5-inch version. I may not catch all that many bass, but the ones I do catch will usually be of much better quality."

Another mistake many anglers make on a numbers lake is using "local favorite" lures, Eaker has found. "If the word gets out that Joe Lunchbucket caught 'em last weekend on a 6-inch purple worm, pretty soon everybody on the lake is throwing the same lure. Small bass are attracted to sheer movement, so they'll bite anything you throw at them. But the bigger bass in the lake are smart — they learn not to strike lures they see time and time again."

Eaker makes a point of finding out which lures the majority of the lake's anglers are using, then fishes something different. "If everybody is throwing a little lipless crankbait, I might use a big spinnerbait, which covers the same band of water but presents a different look and greater mass."

PRACTICING catch-and-release is vital to the future of the sport — especially trophy bass fishing.

TECHNIQUES FOR SPAWNING BASS

Conservation and restraint must be key words when anglers hunt for big, bedding bass

CATCHING HEAVYWEIGHT, roe-laden female bass from spawning beds is as controversial a subject as anything in bass fishing. But like it or not, it's a fact that an extremely high percentage of bass destined for taxidermists each year are caught off nests in spring.

And therein lies the dilemma, as well as the answer, to the age-old hullabaloo surrounding whether or not anglers should catch and keep spawning bass.

"Catching big bass from the nest isn't the most sporting way of fishing, and as a matter of fact, if it were outlawed tomorrow I'd go right along with (the prohibition), because many people don't understand the trophy aspect of 'bed fishing' and can abuse the resource," says 51-year-old Don Brunson of Geneva, Ala. "I'd bet my last nickel that I could catch pretty near every big spawning bass — ones weighing 8 pounds or better — from some of the little lakes I fish if I tried hard enough in spring. And that can really cripple a small lake's big fish population.

"So, if you're gonna fish the beds, you've got to develop what I call a 'trophy attitude.' By that I mean you only keep big bass that you'll take to the taxidermist, because they are genuine trophies — ones that are your personal best during a lifetime of fishing. Every other spawning bass should be released unharmed. If the 'trophy attitude' were in the minds of all anglers who fish for spawning bass, there'd be no problem of injuring fish populations."

Coming from one of the all-time great spawning-bass catchers, such conservationist statements about fishing for bedding bass seem incongruous — until one understands more about Don Brunson, who he is, and what he does.

(Opposite page) KNOWING WHEN to go is the key to catching spawning bass.

Brunson, you see, is just an average fisherman. He doesn't fish bass tournaments. He doesn't belong to a bass club. He doesn't own a bass boat. He fishes close to home. And he'd just as soon catch bream or crappie or

MANY PROS use a tube as their go-to bait for bed fishing.

STEALTH IS a huge factor for catching spawning bass when they are easily spooked in the shallows.

speckled trout as try for bass. Brunson is just an ordinary, south Alabama angler who works long hours at his marina and fishes in his spare time. He's much like 50 million other American anglers in many respects — except for one — Brunson likes to catch heavyweight largemouth bass (on lures, not bait), and he is very good at it.

Brunson learned long ago that the best time for catching truly huge, wallhanger-size largemouth is in spring, when females are heavy with spawn. And over the years, he has discovered the little lakes near his home in south Alabama and the panhandle of Florida that offer the best chances for producing such huge spring fish.

Keep in mind, now, that Brunson doesn't live, eat, sleep and breathe bass fishing, except in spring. Even then, he only gets out a few times each week. But in a 10 year period, Brunson caught 38 largemouth bass weighing 10 pounds or better. Once, in a single night of fishing alone, he boated bass weighing 9 1/2, 10 1/4, 10 1/2, 12 1/2 and 14 pounds!

He has only five mounted bass; each was sent to the taxidermist because at the time, it was the biggest he had landed. They weighed 13 1/2, 14, 14 3/4, 16 1/2, and 18 1/2 pounds! He has released three bass in the 14-pound class, because he has bigger ones on his den wall.

Describing himself as a conservationist, Brunson prefers not to identify the lake he caught the 18 1/2 pounder from for fear this would reveal his fishing spots.

Brunson, a retired Air Force man, and his 21-year-old nephew Steve Kliewer, also of Geneva, were scouting the Panhandle lake one March night. They spotted the big bass as they eased along with the electric motor in Brunson's 14-foot skiff, scanning the bottom and looking for bass nests with a 12-volt, high intensity light.

"The fish spooked off a spawning nest as we slowly moved through the clear shallows," he says. "I knew she was a nice bass, but I only thought she'd weigh 9 or 10 pounds. We were looking for a bass for Steve to catch and mount, and I asked him if he wanted her. He said 'yes,' so we marked the location of the bed, waited 15 minutes, then started casting."

They both used identical all-black, homemade, 7-inch-long soft plastic lizards fitted with 1/4-ounce slip sinkers and 5/0 hooks rigged weedless, Texas style. They repeatedly cast the lizards onto the bass nest to aggravate the fish into striking. Several times the fish hit Steve's lure, and twice it "mouthed" Brunson's artificial. But the bass never took either of the lures deep until it hit Steve's lizard the third time, after about 10 minutes of fishing.

"The third time she hit the lizard I barely tugged on the line — to make her think the lure was trying to escape," Brunson explains. "I guess that made her mad, because she then hit hard and turned fast off the nest to head for deep water. When she did that, I knew she was mine."

With a stiff rod and 25-pound-test line, Brunson set the hook; he immediately knew it was no ordinary largemouth.

"I've hooked bass that have fought more, but that one was so strong and heavy, I just knew it was bigger than the 16-pounder I had mounted," Brunson explains. "She made three or four runs from the boat toward open water, but she never jumped. Twice I thought she'd break the line when I turned her back toward the boat, but everything held. When I worked her in, Steve netted her perfectly.

"Steve reached into the net and grabbed the bass, but couldn't lift it with one hand. I still didn't think the fish was all that big, because it was full dark and I couldn't see her well. But when I lifted her I knew she would go at least 18 pounds."

They put the heavyweight bass in his boat's cooler with two jugs of ice, no water. Brunson wanted to quit fishing and take the bass in for official weighing, but Steve wanted a heavyweight fish, too, so the duo continued fishing until daybreak. They landed several small bass, plus a 6 1/2-pounder and a 9-pounder, but no others anywhere near the size of Brunson's massive fish.

At 7 a.m., the anglers finally left the lake, drove to their hometown and weighed the fish on certified scales at a grocery store in Geneva. Many hours after having been caught, the fish weighed 18 pounds, 8 ounces. There's little doubt the bass dehydrated

SCOUTING OUT **spawning sites can pay off when it matters the most.**

somewhat and lost weight in the dry ice chest. So it's possible the bass could have weighed as much as 19 pounds at the time it was boated.

"For a while there, I didn't think I'd ever catch another bass big enough to mount after I put my 16 1/2-pounder on the wall," Brunson says with a laugh. "Then I get the 18-8, and it's off to the taxidermist again. But I won't mount another one, unless it's bigger than that. It would be hard to release a 16- or 17- or even an 18-pounder, if I catch one again. But I will. It's my 'trophy attitude,' and I have my own conscience to live with. Besides, I know there are some bigger bass than that 18-8 out there. Heck, I've had at least one other fish on I'm sure was in the 20-pound range — but I lost it."

Don Brunson's skills as a big bass fisherman are no secret to some anglers in his area, and he's had people follow him, trying to learn where he fishes and how he catches so many big bass.

"There are plenty of bed fishermen working a lot of the same lakes I do in spring, and they're very good at it," Brunson states. "But there are some secrets — little techniques — to consistently catch truly trophy bass.

"Knowing when to go is a big part of it, especially if you're a working man and the amount of time you can spend fishing is limited. For my area, the best time is the last two weeks of February and the first two weeks of March. Of course, that depends on how low the weather and water temperatures are. For instance, one real warm year, I had my best fishing in January.

PRIVATE WATERS produce high yields during spawning season. Get permission from the landowner before hunting down a trophy in these lightly fished areas.

When it's really cold, late March is good."

Brunson doesn't use a calendar or thermometer to predict when he should try for bedding bass. He lets the fish tell him when to go. He lives just a few miles from one of his favorite lakes, Victor, and uses it as a barometer of the bass spawn.

"I wait until there's a nice warming trend in about late January, and I launch my boat on Victor and ease along the shallows looking for nests," he explains. "The lake is clear and I can see the beds — if they're there. I'll fish a bit and if there's no activity, I'll go home and come back in a few days. When they start bedding on Victor, I know they're spawning on all the other lakes in the area, because they're all pretty much the same size and depth."

"A lot of bed fishermen spend too much time fishing nests that aren't being actively worked by truly trophy largemouth," Brunson explains. "Most of the time, I'll spook the big female off the nest when I'm checking the shallows, and frequently I

Night Moves

won't even bother fishing a bed unless I see her. But I can pretty much tell just by looking at a nest if a big bass is using it. The nest often has debris in or around it — like a log or stump — and it will be a large nest that's kind of rough-looking, not real round and perfectly dished out, like the ones smaller bass make. Most of the time a heavyweight fish will nest in deep water, much deeper than small, 4- to 6-pounders. On my area's lakes, the biggest ones bed in 4 to 6 feet of water, and once I establish the pattern of depth for a few big bass nests, most all of them will be at the same depth. That's helpful to know on waters that are not clear and where beds cannot be seen readily.

"Most of the time the biggest bass will have their nests near very deep water, either right on a dropoff, or close to it. Points are great big bass spawning spots, because the fish have access to deep water on both sides of the nest. A few stumps, stickups and weeds on a point having deep water close by makes the place even more attractive to a trophy spawning largemouth."

Another important technique in catching trophy spawning bass, according to Brunson, is to cast to the nest from shallow water. He maintains that when a bass strikes, it invariably heads to deep water and away from a boat that is anchored on the shallow side of the nest. This is advantageous to the angler, because no slack line will result as it would if the boat were on the deep side of the bed.

Accurate casting is another important aspect of successful bed fishing, Brunson insists, since each unsuccessful cast near a nest alarms the bass and makes it more cautious. He also abides by the old rule of putting the smaller male bass in the livewell should it hit before the larger female bass, which is the case most of the time. And the male always should be released later, even if the female isn't duped into striking. If the male is removed from the nesting site, the female won't return and the angler's chance of catching the big fish is over, says Brunson.

He once caught and released a single male bass more than a dozen times during a 10 day period, before he caught a 13 1/2-pound female bass that was holding on the nest. He then returned the small male bass to the bed.

"Those little buck bass are vital to the successful nesting of the fish on any water, and they should always be released," Brunson emphasizes. "This bed fishing game can be *too* deadly, much too effective for a bass angler's own good — unless he uses plenty of restraint and self-control. You've got to think trophies. Nothing less ever should be taken from the beds."

Although Don Brunson would much rather fish during daylight hours, and often does because of his work schedule, he says night is the best time to catch trophy largemouth from their beds. He's convinced the majority of big bass spawn at night. Two or three days on either side of the full-moon phase is the time he's found the biggest bass to be the most active.

When he begins a night of fishing, he first eases through the shallows with his skiff's electric motor, "shining" the bottom with a high powered light and looking for likely beds to fish. He'll locate four to eight nests, mark them with stakes, then circle back and start casting to them. While fishing, he never uses the big light, just a low powered 2-cell flashlight, and he's careful never to shine it directly on the water — just at the tops of stakes to determine their exact locations.

SHORELINE ANGLING is the best chance to catch a big bass on a fly rod.

HUNTING TROPHIES ON FOOT

Fishing small waters on foot can pay big dividends for the angler seeking the bass of a lifetime

FOR MANY, the term "bass fishing" conjures pictures of a metalflaked bass boat flying across a giant reservoir, and anglers decked out in colorful tournament shirts, putting limits of fish in the livewell. It's a compelling scene, but certainly not the only way to go bass fishing.

The black bass was a gamefish long before the advent of bass boats and graphite rods. When George Perry caught the 22-pound, 4-ounce world record largemouth in 1932, there weren't any depthfinders or trolling motors — not even fiberglass boats. Perry caught his behemoth from a

small skiff, and many other huge bass have been hooked by bank-bound anglers.

Footloose bass fishing gets you into places where, for one reason or another, you can't launch a boat, including small lakes and ponds where anglers are restricted to bank fishing, or in waters lacking launch facilities. Many of these waters have awesome largemouth lurking in them — fish that get little or no pressure from other anglers. They are well worth checking out, even if you have to leave your boat at home.

You'll find other advantages to footloose

bassing: On foot, you can get in a whole weekend of fishing for pennies. It's also a relaxing, low pressure way to fish. And most importantly, it works. Interestingly enough, it can work as well on large bodies of water as it does on small ones.

True, shore anglers on large reservoirs face some restrictions. It's impossible to reach isolated structure features like submerged humps and stream channels positioned more than a cast from the bank, for example. However, plenty of good options remain available along the bank. After all, that's where the majority of bass boat anglers spend most of the day.

At times, it's also where the majority of bass are. If you choose your shore fishing locales properly, you can fish both shallow waters, where bass are relating to such structures as docks and riprap, and deeper structure as well.

A bank angler's best friend is a good topo map that shows him where he can get within casting range of deeper water at the times of the year when bass are deep, and where he can effectively fish the shallows when the bass are there.

Prominent structures in shallow water with deep water nearby have always been a bass magnet. You can usually find a number of such places on any lake, and these are often accessible from the bank. When conditions are right, being on the bank is not a disadvantage; it might actually be a plus.

The footloose fisherman has another advantage over boaters — stealth. The boat that gives the angler mobility also creates a disturbance in the environment that bass — especially trophy class bass — notice. Smaller bass may not react that much, but larger (older, smarter) bass are wary creatures. Many trophy bass specialists who fish from boats resort to double anchoring their craft right on the shoreline to reduce the chance of spooking big fish.

Being on foot not only allows you to concentrate on the area you are fishing — it forces you to do so. Where the average boat angler may give an area two or three casts and then move on, the shore angler can't move quite so fast, so he usually is methodical, covering the area within casting range carefully.

One real advantage of being on foot is that you are properly positioned to fish the bank side of weedbeds. It's amazing how many large bass you'll find on the sheltered side of a big weedline, especially in spring.

Finally, you gain peace and quiet by stepping out of the boat and onto shore. You'll enjoy the slower pace and simplicity of this brand of fishing. It's a laid-back way to fish, most of the time — until that bass of a lifetime latches on and tries to take away your rod and reel.

GO WITH THE BARE essentials when casting for shoreline trophies. Consequently, planning ahead and knowing what to pack is key.

Pack Light For Footloose Fishing

A small tackle pouch, creel or day-bag will hold more than enough tackle and gear. Instead of packing a dozen crankbaits, carry three or four. Cut your selection of soft plastics from hundreds to dozens. Mix in a selection of jigs, spinnerbaits and topwater lures that fit in a couple of smaller plastic boxes, and you're equipped for a day on the shore.

Instead of a half-dozen rods rigged with different lures, you have to rely on one or perhaps two rods while on foot. A medium weight, medium action spinning rod 6 1/2 to 7 feet in length, with a quality monofilament line of 8- to 12-pound test will suffice for most circumstances. The longer rod gives you good casting distance with lightweight lures.

A good backup rod for working the heaviest cover along the shore would be a baitcasting rod rigged with 12- to 20-pound-test line. With this, you can pitch or flip soft plastics and jigs into thick brush and blowdowns that hold big bass, and you'll have some assurance that you'll get your lure back. The baitcaster is also good for those occasions when you want to throw a big swim bait in small waters where big bass mingle with planted trout.

Along with being methodical in your coverage, chances are good you'll concentrate on one or two lures, rather than picking up a different rod every few casts. You'll probably discover quickly that soft plastics and jigs are easily the most effective lures. They don't make a lot of noise and scare bass in the shallows. Also, they retrieve from deep to shallow with fewer hang-ups than crankbaits.

A Carolina rig, which can be cast long distances, makes a great searching bait for the shore angler trying to find fish or cover in a large area. Spinnerbaits and crankbaits are good for scouring an area quickly, although suspending, deep diving crankbaits can be awkward when you're casting into deep water and retrieving through the shallows. A floating/diving model will be easier to handle from shore.

When you have lots of obvious shore structure, or are fishing docks or pilings, Texas rigging a worm is better for short range work and pinpoint accuracy.

LANDING BIG BASS

Knowing how to hook and play fish can make all the difference in whether or not the big one gets away

THE SIGHT OF the feisty 5-pounder both buoyed and sank Roland Martin's emotions in the span of about two seconds.

It was during the heat of the battle in a high stakes BASS event, and time was fleeting. The Florida pro was desperately in need of a decent size largemouth to upgrade his limit catch and become a factor in the tournament. As the hours — and his chances of doing well — were fading fast, Martin was startled by the surface commotion of a big fish that intercepted his jerkbait in the short space between a boat dock and his boat. But his exhilaration soon gave way to anxiety.

"When I got it up to the boat, I could see that one treble hook had it in the side of the gill plate," he recalls. "That was all. Just one little bitty treble hook.

"As the fish came by the boat, I could see the whole plug at right angles to the fish's mouth. I just knew it was going to get off. So I thought if I gave him a lot of slack, maybe he would turn into the plug and somehow get hooked up again. I loosened my drag and played it real light and easy. The fish never did jump; it just kept swimming around. Sure enough, it finally turned just right, and another set of trebles sunk in. Then I could lip the fish."

Relying on years of experience to help him through a nerve-wracking situation, Martin did not panic. Instead, he displayed the steel nerves of a bomb squad technician. And it worked out exactly as planned.

When it comes to landing big bass, the touring pros go to great lengths and resort to various types of stunts to make sure the big one doesn't get away. Give these tactics a try and you will improve the odds of landing the big one.

THE FIGHT

All the pros agree that the most dangerous moments during the battle between bass and man is when the fish decides to jump. A plethora of bad things can happen when a bass is airborne.

But the brightest minds in professional fishing disagree on how to avoid these tense moments.

"It's important to understand why a bass jumps," says Texas angler Randy Fite. "They tend to jump because people exert a lot of pressure on them, and the only way a fish can ease that pressure is to come up. So by going easy on the fish, it will tend to turn back down and start 'dogging.' As long as it can take a little line once in a while, the fish will keep its

head down and won't come up to jump."

The most common tactic the pros rely on to discourage hooked bass from jumping is to thrust the tip of the rod beneath the surface of the water. The success rate of this technique is questionable.

"When you've got a fish on, watch your line, and you will often be able to tell whether it's going to jump," top pro Alton Jones instructs. "If the fish is way out at the end of a long cast, I will stick my rod in the water and reel as hard as I can to try to pull his head down as soon as it comes up.

"When the fish gets close to the boat, though, I won't put my rod tip in the water. If it decides to jump within a couple of feet of the boat, I may

never let him get his head back in the water. I may just use the momentum of his jump to swing the fish in the boat."

If a bass jumps, South Carolina pro Davy Hite emphasizes that it's better to have it occur well away from the boat while the angler has plenty of line out. Most fatal mistakes occur when the fish vaults out of the water near the boat on a short line — then, line stretch becomes a critical factor.

Martin, who fishes with braided line, points out that the relatively new superlines have virtually no stretch and are particularly vulnerable to bass that jump and struggle at boatside. That's why he uses a length of monofilament as a leader in most situations.

ANTICIPATING THE
fish's next move is
important when play-
ing it near the boat.
Move the rod in the
direction the fish is
headed, instead of
getting into a tug-
ging match.

Jones offers three tips for surviving the battle with any trophy bass.

"One thing that helped me negotiate the tricky parts of landing a big fish was real-
izing that whatever direction you pull on a bass, it will try to go in the opposite direction. A lot of times, if you actually pull a big fish toward that bush on the left, it will
swim away from the cover and out into open water. Pulling in the opposite direction
you want the fish to go really works.

"Another thing I do when I hook a big fish on a bait with treble hooks and know
it's away from the cover, is immediately back off the drag. By backing off the drag, I
reduce the risk of the fish using its strength to pull off the treble hooks.

"When a bass gets hung up in an underwater brushpile or some other cover I can't see,
I have found that giving it a little slack will often encourage it to swim back out of the
cover. I'm not talking about free spooling the reel, just stop pulling on the fish and keeping your line somewhat tight with your rod. You should barely be able to feel the fish."

SWEEPING CHANGES

With fast moving lures like crankbaits, jerkbaits and spinnerbaits, Ohio pro Joe
Thomas often makes sweeping motions with his rod from one side to the other during
the fight to gain the upper hand with big bass.

"We're using soft rods and stretchy line and sharp hooks to keep it from tearing
out, but to get more hooks in the fish, you have to be going against the grain of the
fish," he explains. "In other words, if the fish is running from right to left, you need to

Landing Methods

Landing nets are banned in high-level BASS tournaments. Many pros prefer to land their fish by hand, anyway, reasoning that waiting for a partner to grab the net jeopardizes finishing the job.

Whenever possible, Roland Martin recommends lip-landing a big bass. He calls that the surest technique of all for boating a sizable bass.

Davy Hite's recommendations depend upon the type of lure involved. For treble-adorned lures like jerkbaits, crankbaits and topwater plugs, Hite always uses his off hand to either lip or "belly land" those fish. With single-hook baits, like jigs and soft plastics, he routinely swings them into the boat.

To swing or not to swing is often a crucial decision.

"I won't swing one over, say, 5 pounds," Hite continues. "Even then, I have to know how the fish is hooked.

"If it is hooked outside the jaw, I know I'd better get it in quickly because I'm likely to lose that fish. I'll use its momentum as it comes toward the boat and quickly swing it in."

If a fish seems to have the entire jig or worm in its mouth, that's not necessarily a sign the fish is well-hooked, Hite warns. "A lot of times, the jig is just skin-hooked in the roof of the mouth, and it will tear loose when you try to swing that bass into the boat."

Alton Jones points out several other considerations when determining whether a bass is a likely candidate to be swung over the gunwale: The amount and direction of the bass' momentum at the time, the size of the hook(s) and the species on the end of the line.

Like a growing number of fishermen, Jones prefers to belly-land smallmouth and spotted bass — as well as any fish that has "a face full of trebles." After tiring the bass, Jones grasps the line with one hand and lies on his back so he can slide the fish into the open palm of his other hand. Surprisingly, the bass seems to relax at this moment, allowing the angler to lift it into the boat.

"It's amazing how docile bass get when you grab their belly gently," Jones says. "I never would have guessed that a fish would react like that."

ADVOCATES OF belly-landing contend this method relaxes the fish, thereby making it easier to land by hand.

sweep your rod to the right. You're trying to pull the line across the fish at all times. That way, if the lure starts to pop free, you have a chance of hooking it again or having another hook stick into it."

Top Texas pro Dean Rojas emphasizes that more big bass are lost at boatside than during any other portion of the fight.

"Once you get them up close to the boat, that's when your rod skills really come into play, and you need to know how to control the rod and the drag while leading the fish around," says Rojas. "You always want to figure out what the fish is going to do next. If you see it darting around in front of the boat, you always want to go with it. Don't ever sit there and get into a tugging match with it, because you're going to lose about 80 percent of the time.

"When a fish makes a lunge or a run, I like to go with it as if I'm giving in to the fish. I might 'bow' to the fish like tarpon fishermen do, or I'll kneel to give it more line if it's running deep. The keys are to work a fish as easily as you can and to make sure your drag is set right. A lot of times, I'll even adjust my drag while I'm fighting a big fish on light line. It's important to let the bass swim and tire itself out."

THE BENEFIT of a replica mount is the fish is released and can be caught again.

REPLICA MOUNTS: TROPHY BASS LIFESAVERS

Thanks to fish artists like these, you can release your catch and still hang 'it' on your wall

SURE, ANYONE ON any given day can catch a trophy bass, but it takes a dedicated conservationist to resist the temptation of keeping that once-in-a-lifetime catch and taking it to the taxidermist.

It's not a cardinal sin to kill a big bass and have it "stuffed" for hanging on the wall of your den. But advancements in replica taxidermy make it possible — even preferable — to let that fish swim away.

For example, to be admitted to the Bassmaster Lunker Club, an angler must catch a largemouth bass weighing 10 or more pounds, or a smallmouth bass weighing 6 pounds or more. However, to have the photo of his big bass published in *Bassmaster*, the angler must also release the fish alive.

Increasingly, Lunker Club applicants are choosing to have replica mounts made to commemorate their achievements.

In the past, phony-looking fiberglass reproductions were the only option for anglers wanting to release their trophy fish. Now, catch-and-release advocates can have lifelike replicas made of their memorable catches.

Some reproduction mounts of trophy bass from Lunker Club participants have been made by Don's Taxidermy of Smithville, Mo. Owner Don Frank estimates his business creates more than 100 replica fish mounts a year. He has noticed an increase in the demand for reproduction mounts, which he attributes to the practice of catch-and-release and an awareness of increased fishing pressure.

"Fishermen realize that if 7-, 8-, 9- or 10-pound fish are taken out on a regular basis, there is no way the fishery can sustain itself with that amount of fishing pressure," says Frank.

This awareness has created a dramatic rise in Frank's replica business. "Five years ago, replica mounts made up 5 to 10 percent of my business; now it's pushing half," says Frank, who has been a full-time taxidermist for 20 years.

Orders for reproduction mounts also have increased over the years at Archie Phillips Taxidermy in Alabama. "It is a growing part of the industry," says Phillips.

(Opposite page) USING A REPUTABLE taxidermist will provide you with a replica that looks like the real thing.

MEASURE THE length and the girth of a trophy smallmouth, and provide the information to a taxidermist. In doing so, you can release the fish after taking its picture.

The veteran taxidermist believes Alabama's numerous farm ponds (more than 47,000) have helped his replica business. "When a fellow owns a pond and wants to raise big fish, he knows he can catch one from his pond and turn the fish back in," says Phillips. "So, he can get a reproduction of the fish and maybe catch that fish again the next year."

Replica mounts of six bass, which Missouri angler Dan Boyer says is an unofficial state record limit, hang on a wall at his home. After photographing and measuring each fish, Boyer released all the bass into the subdivision lake he was fishing. The measurements and photographs helped Brad Bilbrey of Bilbrey Studio Taxidermy in Barnhart, Mo., reproduce Boyer's memorable catch in fiberglass.

The Missouri taxidermist works mostly on skin mounts, which Bilbrey can make cheaper than replicas. His major expense for a replica mount is the fiberglass blank, which he has to order from a supplier. "It's unfortunate, because a lot of guys will keep that fish to save a hundred bucks," says Bilbrey. "There is no fish that is any better-looking than a fiberglass mount. Once you finish it and hang it on the wall, it's like painting a car hood. It's going to look exactly like that forever."

Frank has a small inventory of his own casts, but he, too, depends mostly on existing blanks from suppliers. "It gives me a lot larger selection to pull from, and I have access to all the new casts the replica companies are making," he says.

Improvements in the blanks make today's replica mounts look more realistic. "In the last 10 years, there have been several new reproduction companies that are using better materials and techniques in order to cast the fish," discloses Frank. "Now, the quality of the better replicas is good enough that most people can't tell that they are replicas."

A limited number of blanks remains the main drawback of reproduction mounts, though. "There are a lot of misnomers about how they are made. A lot of guys think we just make them from scratch and put all the detail in ourselves, which is not the case," says Frank. "They have no idea what a taxidermist has to do to make one. In order to make a replica mount, someone has to have caught a fish that size, so a mold is made of that fish. Your catch ends up being an exact duplicate of another fish that size."

Even though he makes his own blanks, Phillips still incurs a major cost when he has to keep adding molds for various sizes of fish. "Every now and then, one will come along that we don't have, so we'll make a mold of that. It's a never-ending thing," says Phillips, who has about 1,000 molds in his supply. His reproduction mounts cost approximately $250 for an 8-pound bass, whereas a skin mount for the same size fish is about $150.

The Alabama taxidermist creates more than 1,000 replica bass mounts a year. Phillips, one of the pioneers of fiberglass mounts, started making replica mounts of

MISSOURI ANGLER DAN BOYER measured and took photos of each fish to have reproduction mounts made of this heavy-weight limit of bass, which he caught and released at a subdivision lake.

saltwater fish almost 40 years ago. He has definitely seen the long-term benefits of his reproductions.

"With a replica, you'll never have any aging or cracking problems that you sometimes encounter with skin mounts," says Phillips. "Over time, if you get too much heat or humidity, sometimes skin mounts will crack around the scales, whereas a fiberglass reproduction is forever."

The taxidermist's job of making an exact replica becomes easier if anglers gather some vital information about their trophy catch before releasing it. The weight of a trophy catch is all Phillips requires to make a replica mount. He believes most bass in the same weight class are similar in length.

"That's particularly true of smallmouth — you can almost stamp them out of a mold," says Phillips. "You can have a little different problem with a largemouth, because some of the fish have extended girths. Spotted bass also run like smallmouth. If they get around 6 or 7 pounds, they get a potbelly."

Frank and Bilbrey recommend taking a good photograph and measuring the bass' length and girth for the most precise replica mount. "If you measure length and girth, I can usually get within an inch either way of that, unless you have a real oddball fish," Bilbrey says.

A flexible tape works best for measuring your trophy catch. If a measuring device is unavailable, photographs taken in proper proportions also can determine the length of a trophy fish. "You see guys who, when they catch big fish, the first thing they do for a picture is stretch their arms out and hold that fish out as far as they can," says Bilbrey. "That way, in the photograph the fish actually looks 6 or 8 inches bigger than it really is." The taxidermist suggests taking some photos of your catch while holding it next to your leg or other objects (tackleboxes or fishing rods), so he can measure later to scale the size of the fish.

Today's realistic replica mounts have become real lifesavers for trophy bass. The ranks of the Bassmaster Lunker Club might grow considerably if more anglers realize they can release their once-in-a-lifetime catch and still hang a precise copy of it on their walls.

Tips for Trophy Fish Replicas

When you're fishing in trophy territory and think you might want a replica mount of your catch, be prepared.

■ Include a camera with a flash and an accurate scale in your fishing gear. Weigh the fish and get good photos. Use the flash during bright midday sun or cloudy, poor light conditions.

■ Measure the fish's length. Some taxidermists might like to have an accurate girth measurement as well. Provided with a photo, a good taxidermist can match the fish to a corresponding replica size. Most taxidermists would rather have a photo and a weight than a girth measurement. If you don't have a measuring tape, Texas bass guide Lindy Roberts recommends cutting a piece of monofilament to match the fish's length, and another piece to match its girth. "I give the length and girth-measuring lines to the fisherman and make him put them in his wallet for safekeeping," Roberts says.

■ Handle the fish carefully for photos and measurements. Put the fish in a livewell or, better yet, hold it in the water until you're ready with the camera and scales. Roberts first photographs the fish with a Polaroid so the client has a photo he can take with him for instant gratification. He then snaps a few quick shots with a 35 mm camera. He quickly measures and weighs the fish before releasing it. "I can hold my breath during the whole process," says Roberts. Bass handled carefully and released immediately stand a good chance of surviving the experience. If you hold the fish out of water for five minutes while you locate and load the camera, you may as well kill it and have a skin mount.

Before selecting a taxidermist to do your replica, check out other replicas he's done, just to make certain the work is suitable. Another good thing about a fish replica is that there's no rush to get the fish to a convenient taxidermy shop. You can even phone in the order, once you've settled on a taxidermist.

SECRETS FOR BIG SMALLMOUTH

Use this inside information to land

a big bronzeback . . .

USING BIG BAITS doesn't necessarily mean you alienate small bass. Aggressive smallies, even small ones, will hit large lures.

BIG BAITS EQUAL BIG SMALLMOUTH

Want to catch trophy smallmouth? Leave the little lures at home

A REVOLUTION IS taking place. On rivers and lakes all over the country, smallmouth bass anglers are learning that bigger is better. Instead of throwing 3-inch grubs, tiny crankbaits and little in-line spinners, recreational anglers are following the lead of professional anglers who need big bass. Whether it's to catch the heaviest limit of fish or to help a client boat the biggest smallmouth of his life, smallmouth experts are swapping traditional lures for bigger, meatier baits designed for largemouth.

BIG, FLASHY AND TRASHY

Bill Kramer, a smallmouth guide on the Susquehanna and upper Potomac rivers, has been catching bruiser smallmouth bass on big baits all his life. The first few, he admits, were by accident.

"My father and grandfather and I would throw big spinnerbaits for pike in Minnesota," recalls Kramer. "We caught some unbelievable smallmouth along with the pike, so it didn't take us long to figure out that we had a new way to catch big smallmouth."

He took that method back home and tried it on the Susquehanna River, where most anglers threw the standard fare for smallmouth. Many still do. It worked so well that Kramer regularly uses big, gaudy spinnerbaits that most anglers reserve for largemouth bass.

"I still have a hard time convincing some of my clients that these great big spinnerbaits will 'kill' big smallmouth," he says, "but once they catch that first big bass, they won't put it down."

Not surprisingly, New Jersey pro and BASS world champion Mike Iaconelli also discovered that big lures account for some hefty stringers of smallmouth bass. Like Kramer, he spent much of his boyhood casting big in-line spinners and spinnerbaits to pike and pickerel, and he discovered that huge bass slammed those oversize baits as

(Opposite page) BRONZEBACK ANGLERS fishing in weedy cover favor big soft jerkbaits.

MOVING WATER and rock is the magical combination for river smallmouth.

TROPHY TIME FOR RIVER SMALLIES

For the smallmouth of a lifetime, visit a bronzeback river in early winter

THE 2 1/2-POUND BRONZEBACK Mark Agner corralled from the cold waters of Virginia's New River was indeed a nice one, but Agner barely noted its presence.

An hour or so later, however, the Virginia schoolteacher did connect with a fish that quickened the pulse of even this dedicated trophy hunter. Agner's 6 1/2-pounder weighed within a pound of the standing Old Dominion state record of 7 pounds, 7 ounces.

Agner has threatened breaking the state record before — and he's likely to do so again — all in a season when most anglers have given up river fishing for the year.

Much has been written about the best times to seek out trophy river smallmouth. But for Agner, one very specific time and certain very specific methods are all that matter.

"The early winter period, especially in December, when the water temperature ranges between 48 and 54 degrees, is the prime time to go after really big smallmouth," says Agner, who teaches physical education at Lord Botetourt High School in Daleville. "I think larger smallmouth have to feed longer into the winter than smaller ones do, because their metabolism demands it. Their bigger bodies need more food in preparation for winter."

Agner concentrates his search for trophies in one specific type of area — long, deep pools.

The subtle characteristics of a prime pool are what make it a likely haunt for lunkers. For example, the spot that produced that 6 1/2-pound smallmouth also has given him two other fish almost as heavy.

This pool is just a quarter-mile long from riffle to riffle, and it is situated in the bend of a river. Upstream from the lower riffle exists a long, shallow shelf ranging from 1 to 5 feet under water. And at the upstream edge of that shelf is a dropoff that plunges sharply into 10 or 12 feet of water. That dropoff continues for a number of yards and then the river bottom once again rises up to within a few feet of the surface. Finally, the upstream riffle signals the end of the pool.

The very pronounced dropoff naturally holds big smallmouth in late fall and early winter — a period when fish require deep sanctuaries they can retreat to when the water temperature or weather conditions change suddenly, notes Agner. On some rivers, he says, even deeper water may be required to hold big bronze-backs. The key is to look for dropoffs into water that is 4 or 5 feet deeper than the "average" depth of the stream. And once you zero in on a dropoff, seek out basketball-size rocks or submerged trees — prime lairs for big bass.

Agner adds that early winter smallmouth hold at or near those ledges more than 90 per-cent of the time. Besides the overgrown bass, baitfish and large gamefish also dwell in this same area. Since the water in the pool remains well-oxygenated from the upstream riffles and is sta-ble in flow because of the ledge's damming effect, there is literally no need for bass to venture far for food or comfort.

Agner is as particular about the bait he offers these big bass as he is the structure in which he seeks them. He relies solely on chubs and suckers at least 6 inches long.

"Those soft-rayed fish are the most natural prey of river bass, and fishing with larger baits prevents rock bass and small bass from messing with it," he says.

"To get the most out of chubs and suckers, you also have to work them naturally, and that means fishing them downstream from the back of your anchored boat," he

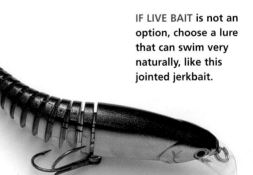

IF LIVE BAIT is not an option, choose a lure that can swim very naturally, like this jointed jerkbait.

MARK AGNER believes that late fall and early winter are perhaps the best times to catch a trophy river smallmouth.

explains. "Most fishermen prefer to cast live bait upstream and let it drift back with the current. Although that approach sounds good in theory, in reality, bait presented that way tends to ride up in the current and move out of a bass' strike zone. By casting a bait downstream, I also have more control of it."

Agner maintains that control by tightlining his offerings. Periodically, he lifts his rod tip from the 9 o'clock position to 12 o'clock, making his bait rise 3 feet off the bottom, and then he lets out 4 feet of line. The effect is of a struggling baitfish trying to swim above the bottom and then vulnerably drifting back in the current a few feet. Hits typically occur when the baitfish rises from the bottom or begins to settle downward.

He rigs a chub or sucker on an size 2 Eagle Claw Model 42 hook, which is a wide gap hook. He ties it to the line with a Palomar knot, and he runs the hook through the upper half of the fish's mouth and out a nostril. This approach allows the bait to swim in an unrestricted manner.

About 2 feet up the line, Agner affixes a Size 5 to 7 round split shot (removable shot with "lips" hang up too much), depending on the strength of the current. Interestingly, he utilizes relatively light line.

"I prefer Cabella's Platinum line in 8-pound test," Agner explains. "This line duplicates the color of the sky, which is what the fish see when they look up. Green line, for example, may seem to disappear when you are looking down on it from a boat. But to a fish, that shade of line, and other colors as well, look out of place.

"Some people like 20-pound test or so for trophy fishing. But heavy line won't sink as well as light line does. And it also doesn't allow the bait to move realistically. You should muscle a big smallmouth with your rod, not with your line."

To do so, Agner relies on 6 1/2-foot medium/heavy baitcasting rod rated for 8- to 17-pound test. The drag is set as loose as possible while the baitfish is being worked through a pool. When a fish strikes, Agner free-spools the line, tightens the drag, reels in slack and sets the hook. If an overgrown bass makes a move for a snag, Agner uses the stout rod to turn the fish.

With such big baits, Agner doesn't expect to have more than one or two hits in a day's time. For example, on the day his most recent trophy was subdued, he and his boat partner experienced only two bites.

Obviously, great patience is required. Agner often anchors in one spot for as long as 90 minutes — and when he does move, it may be only to drift downstream for 10 yards or so. In 10 hours on the river, he may frequent only two or three pools, working each one thoroughly and repeatedly throughout the day.

His johnboat is outfitted in a Spartan manner, equipped only with a 10-hp outboard, a trolling motor, a livewell and a depthfinder. The sonar is used to pinpoint dropoffs or underwater cover if a river is discolored.

"If you take up trophy fishing during the late fall/early winter period, don't expect to catch a lot of bass," Agner concludes. "But I am convinced that the next Virginia state record could well be caught during that time and from the type of place I fish. And the same thing holds true, I believe, on smallmouth rivers in other states.

"I do strongly recommend, however, that if you catch a trophy, you should take pains to release it. In a river system, a smallmouth takes years to reach trophy size. It would be a real shame to kill a fish like that."

Gathering Bait

Interestingly, Mark Agner catches his chubs and suckers not with a net, but with a hook. He employs a tiny Size 10 hook, on which a little sliver of nightcrawler is impaled. He begins his wintertime bait search in the summer, explaining that chubs and suckers are impossible to catch after the first of November.

Once caught, these baitfish are stored in a "spring house" until needed. For those who can't buy or catch suckers and chubs, jumbo shiners (available at many tackle shops) are possible substitutes. But generally, Agner emphasizes, soft-rayed fish native to the river you fish are the best choices.

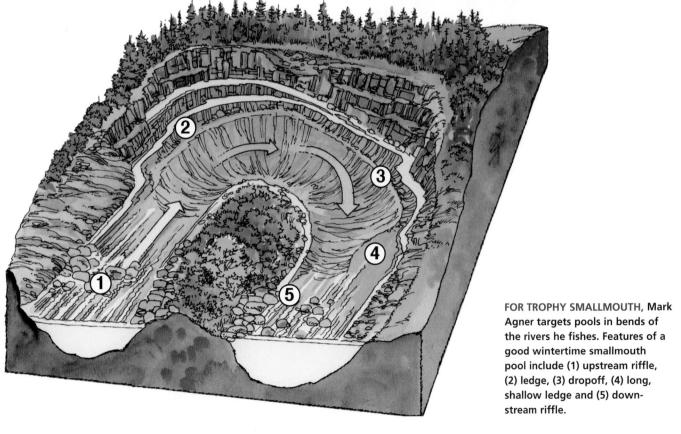

FOR TROPHY SMALLMOUTH, Mark Agner targets pools in bends of the rivers he fishes. Features of a good wintertime smallmouth pool include (1) upstream riffle, (2) ledge, (3) dropoff, (4) long, shallow ledge and (5) downstream riffle.

DESTINATIONS

Your trophy bass trip planner
is here . . .

WHERE TO CATCH THE BASS OF YOUR DREAMS

These seven lakes head the list of hot spots for catching trophy largemouth

OVER THE PAST THREE DECADES, literally dozens of lakes throughout the nation have produced largemouth bass weighing more than 10 pounds. And, as fisheries personnel continue to learn more about trophy bass management, more are added to the list each year.

Far fewer lakes, however, continue to produce big bass on a regular basis year after year, which is really the true measure of a trophy fishery. Given the unpredictable nature of the largemouth bass, even the very best lakes sometimes go through a "drought period" in which 10-pounders seem to disappear. However, the following seven lakes offer some of the best chances in the United States to catch a truly big bass.

The first thing many anglers will notice is that none of the famed San Diego area lakes are included here. Even though several 20-pound fish have been caught in these waters, the lakes' small size, very heavy fishing pressure and limited access preclude listing them. Lake Hodges, for example, which has produced fish heavier than 20 pounds, contains 1,234 acres and is open just three days a week (sunrise to sunset) between early March and late October; most of the other lakes are much smaller and operate under schedules just as confining.

Compare these lakes to Clear Lake, Calif.; Toledo Bend, Texas; and Rodman Reservoir, Fla. — all much larger and open day and night year-round, so pressure is more spread out, and each of which has given up bass in excess of 15 pounds. Studying these statistics, your chances of catching a big bass may actually be better on the larger lakes.

If you do decide to visit any of these lakes, take the time to plan your trip very carefully. On virtually all lakes, there are good, better and best times of the year to visit.

Even in ideal weather, trophy bass fishing requires a great deal of patience and a willingness to go for hours or days with just a few strikes. If you intend to hire a local guide, reserve your days with him as far in advance as possible.

CLEAR LAKE, CALIF.

This 43,000-acre spring-fed lake located near the city of Clearlake, approximately three hours north of San Francisco, has produced bass top-

ping 17 1/2 pounds, along with many in the 8- to 13-pound range. Characterized by a mixture of weedy shoreline cover, boat docks and deep water, Clear Lake is the largest natural lake in the state.

The majority of trophy bass are caught between March and June, and again in October and November. Sight fishing is popular and productive in the clear, spring-fed waters during these months, but during the summer, anglers must share the water with crowds of water-skiers and pleasure boaters.

Favorite big bass areas include Lakeside County Park, with its hydrilla, rocks and tules; Redman Slough, the lake's only tributary; and Konocti Bay, where the bottom contains not only scattered vegetation, but also gravel and rock. BASS pro Byron Velvick won a California tournament here with an incredible catch of 15 bass weighing 83 pounds.

Velvick used one of the famous California swim baits to catch his fish, but equally impressive hauls

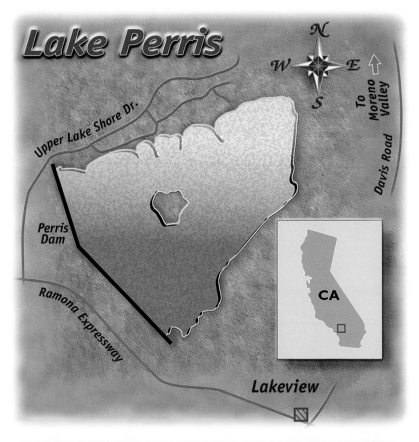

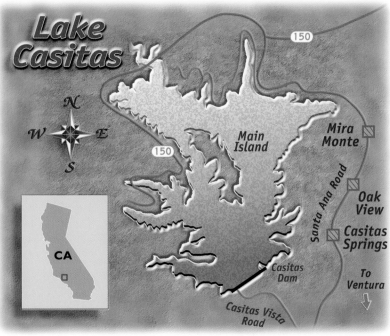

are made with tube jigs, plastic worms, buzzbaits and even crankbaits.

LAKE PERRIS, CALIF.

This 2,600-acre lake, located about 70 miles east of Los Angeles, undoubtedly ranks as one of the state's premier trophy bass lakes. Some have described Perris as the best lake in the United States for bass in the 12- to 15-pound range. Interestingly, this is the California lake famous for its trophy spotted bass fishery, which flourished, then faded after Florida largemouth were introduced.

What makes Perris such an excellent fishery is the combination of water quality, abundant forage, deep breaklines and a variety of cover. Depending on water levels, anglers here can often choose between laydowns, tules, isolated rockpiles and boulders, and even artificial tire reefs. Locally famous trophy bass fishing areas include Allessandro Island, Rock Climber Cove and Rock'N Hole. Each of these spots features rocks and dropoffs into deep water.

Most trophy bass are caught between November and April, which corresponds to the state trout stocking schedule. Naturally, swim baits that imitate trout produce well, as do large plastic worms (often fished on 12-pound line with a 1/8-ounce sinker), jigs and deep diving crankbaits.

LAKE CASITAS, CALIF.

This scenic 2,800-acre lake near Ventura has produced fish heavier than 21 pounds, and some feel it could produce the next world record. That's because unlike many other trophy lakes in California, Casitas offers a lot of shallow water with excellent cover. Casitas also has excellent deeper structure, as well as heavy autumn/winter stockings of rainbow trout.

The majority of big bass are caught between December and March, and many of them come from Orchard Point, Arrow Island and Deer Slope. Each of these spots offers not only shallow spawning flats, but also fast falling drops into much deeper water.

Without question, swim baits rank high on the

list of popular lures here; both trolling and drifting them along the edges of the dropoffs can be productive. Other lure choices include plastic worms, tube jigs and deep crankbaits.

LAKE FORK, TEXAS

No lake in recent years has received as much publicity as this 27,000-acre impoundment north of Mineola. Opened in 1980 and managed specifically to produce trophy bass, Fork has been an unqualified success, having produced seven bass over 16 pounds, including the state record of 18.18 pounds; and at least 30 other fish topping 14 pounds.

Much of this success can be attributed to strict management that includes a protective slot limit of 14 to 24 inches, a strong catch-and-release ethic among local guides, and abundant cover. Until 1999, Lake Fork had a heavy growth of hydrilla that provided almost year-round cover for bass; that vegetation is now beginning to return, and it should be thick and plentiful by the spring of 2002. The lake is also filled with standing timber and brush.

Key fishing areas include some of the various tributary streams flowing into Fork, many of which continually produce the largest bass year after year. Included on this list are Caney, Birch, Mustang, Little Mustang and Blade creeks.

February, March and April are popular fishing months because bass are spawning, but May and June can be excellent because bass tend to gather in larger schools off deep structure. September and October often produce schooling action near the mouths of some of the creeks, with big fish starting to appear again in November and December.

The most popular big bass lure on Fork is a 1/2- or 3/4-ounce jig, but spinnerbaits, plastic worms and lizards (on a Carolina rig), and deep diving crankbaits have all caught big bass.

TOLEDO BEND RESERVOIR, TEXAS/LA.

Recently, during a three month period between late January and late April, at least 17 bass weigh-

Top Trophy Bass Lakes 1997-2001

Lake	Trophies Caught
Lake Fork, Texas	46
Clear Lake, Calif.	25
Lake Walk-in-Water, Fla.	20
Lake Guerrero, Mexico	18
Stick Marsh/Farm 13, Fla.	17
Lake El Salto, Mexico	15
Lake Comedero, Mexico	14
Lake Istokpoga, Fla.	10
Lake Perris, Calif.	10
San Pablo, Calif.	8

Top Trophy Bass States And Countries

State	Trophies Caught
Florida	150
California	127
Texas	101
Mexico	55
North Carolina	22
Louisiana	18
Arizona	18
Georgia	15
Alabama	13
Virginia	12

ing more than 10 pounds were registered at different marinas on Toledo Bend. The largest fish recorded tipped the scales at 14 pounds, 11 ounces — proof that this massive 186,000-acre lake on the Texas/Louisiana border is ready to take its place among the nation's trophy bass producers.

Never before in its 35 year history was Toledo Bend known for trophy bass. It has always been a "numbers lake," producing tons of bass in the 4- to 6-pound range. Now, however, extensive stocking of Florida bass by Texas and Louisiana is finally beginning to pay off.

Anglers familiar with the lake also point out that despite its age, Toledo Bend continues to offer excellent habitat, water quality and fairly light fishing pressure. That's due in part to its size — the lake stretches 65 miles from end to end and contains more than 1,200 miles of shoreline — and its remoteness from major cities. The water is full of stumps, hydrilla, ditches and channels, submerged ridges and sharp depth changes.

Jigs are probably the top lure choices here; in fact, the first "grass jigs" were developed on this lake. Other popular and productive lures include crankbaits, spinnerbaits, Carolina rigged lizards, and Texas rigged worms and tube jigs. February through May are prime months, but double-digit fish also are caught in the fall.

RODMAN RESERVOIR, FLA.

This 10,000-acre Oklawaha River impoundment near the city of Palatka has been producing trophy largemouth for more than 25 years, and despite heavy pressure, it continues to give up numerous big bass every year. In the big bass month of March, a 17-pound, 2-ounce fish was caught here, and a few days later, a 15-2 was brought in.

Although just 13 miles in length, Rodman is filled with standing timber and stumps as well as several different types of vegetation — including hydrilla, bulrush and hyacinth. Forage, especially golden shiners, is also abundant, and the Oklawaha channel offers deeper water adjacent to the cover.

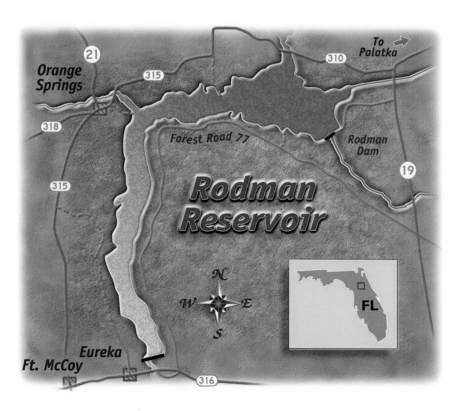

Where To Catch A Lunker

Florida remains the world's hot spot for trophy bass, according to records from more than 600 entries in the Bassmaster Lunker Club.

The Lunker Club is open to BASS members who catch a largemouth bass weighing at least 10 pounds, or a smallmouth weighing 6 pounds or more.

A total of 150 trophy bass from Florida were accepted during the first five years of the Lunker Club's existence, ranking Florida ahead of California, with 127 entries, and Texas, with 101. Mexico ranked fifth, with 55 lunkers.

Almost half of Texas' lunkers came from Lake Fork, which produced 46 bass over 10 pounds in the past five years. California's Clear Lake ranked second among trophy bass factories with 25, while Lake Walk-in-Water, Fla., was third, with 20. Lake Guerrero was fourth in the ranking, although two newer Mexico lakes, El Salto and Comedero, finished in the Top 10 with 15 and 14 bass, respectively. Neither of the latter two lakes was mentioned in Lunker Club entries prior to 2000.

While it's tempting to plan a trip to one of those exotic locales, the best fishing of all may be in your own back yard. Ten percent of trophy bass accepted into the Lunker Club since 1997 have come from private ponds and lakes.

Trophy bass fishing in Florida lakes, of course, centers around the use of live shiners, and Rodman is no exception. During the prime November to March season, shiners frequently have to be reserved in advance at area bait shops. Those who use artificials catch most of their big bass on plastic worms, lizards and soft jerkbaits hopped and crawled along the edges of the vegetation.

While giant bass have been caught on lures, most guides focus on live bait. For whatever reason, whenever the bass are on a shiner bite, artificials like plastic worms and lipless crankbaits seldom get a second look. November through March are considered the best months, although big fish are caught throughout the year.

STICK MARSH, FLA.

Located approximately 25 miles south of Melbourne near the small town of Fellsmere, this catch-and-release fishery has made more than a few trophy dreams come true. Numerous bass in the 12- to 14-pound range have been caught here.

Stick Marsh and the adjoining Farm 13 (which together total 6,700 acres) are actually water retention reservoirs designed to correct siltation problems in the St. Johns River, but after being stocked with Florida bass in 1987, they soon began producing exceptional fishing.

Essentially, anglers here are fishing a flooded forest, swamp and former citrus grove. While trees and brush dominate the landscape above the surface, a surprising number of submerged canals and deeper holes can be found below the surface. Hydrilla and other vegetation also are present.

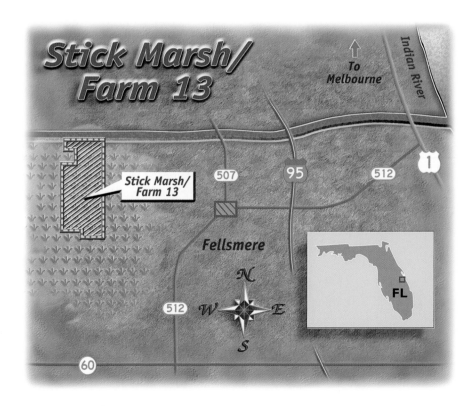

BIG BASS BRAGGIN' RIGHTS

Where will the next world record largemouth be caught? Read this, then place your bets

WHEN MOST BASS FISHERMEN refer to trophy bass, the scale starts at 10 pounds. This is the magical figure that makes heads turn, conversations stop and even the most jaded angler give a begrudging tip of the cap. It's the universal yardstick for bass fishing success. Well, nearly universal.

(Opposite page) IT TAKES BASS in the "teens," like this 13 1/2-pounder, to turn heads in California.

There are certain places in this country where a 10-pound bass doesn't make the local fish report. Where it doesn't cause a ripple of recognition or raise even an inquisitive eyebrow. These are the states where bass fishermen have raised the ante, upped the stakes and, in the current vernacular, "restructured" our thinking when it comes to trophy bass. These are the states where a 10-pounder is still a worthy adversary, but hardly a reason for chest-thumping braggadocio. Places where you just don't swagger up to a group of bass fishermen talking trash about your 10-pounder. For that kind of display, you better have one in the teens. The high teens.

These bass in the trophy class have long sparked our collective imaginations as bass fishermen. Like a *Micropterus salmoides* government lottery, the three states that have tantalized us with dreams of the big payoff, touch saltwater on all three coasts: California, Florida and Texas.

On the record, biologists from the three states quickly nix the notion of any formal three-way competition, and their history of mutual cooperation in sharing information and brood stock confirms that to be true. But to think that these guys don't puff their chests out once in a while is pushing it.

Dennis Lee, a senior fish biologist for California and someone who has had the most to crow about in recent years, admits that whenever the Golden State produces a giant, Allen Forshage of Texas Parks and Wildlife hears about it.

The phone lines run both ways, admits Forshage. "Yes, Texas has always been a bragging state," he says. "We would love to say we have the world record largemouth bass. Right now, we would just like to say we produced a 20-pound bass."

IN TEXAS, sunfish are the forage of choice for big bass. To catch a Lone Star State lunker, choose a bait that resembles this food source.

MANY OF MEXICO'S top lakes cover inundated, overgrown farmland and hold a wealth of bass fishing cover.

FANTASY BASS FISHING SOUTH OF THE BORDER

Double-digit lunkers are commonplace on these four hot Mexican lakes

MEXICO, SPECIFICALLY CANCUN, is renowned as a vacation paradise. Spring-breakers, honeymooners and snowbirds flock by the thousands to this tropical paradise to worship the sun and indulge themselves in food, fun and relaxation.

Bass fishermen escape to Mexico for many of the same reasons, although the prime attraction is the trophy bass fishing. The trophies lurking in Mexico lakes are the stuff that bass fishing dreams are made of. Ten-pounders galore inhabit these waters and are caught so frequently they barely make the bragging board at the resorts dotting their shorelines.

What follows is a rundown on the top trophy lakes in Mexico.

LAKE EL SALTO

Located in the state of Sinoloa about 90 minutes northeast of the port city of Mazatlan, Lake El Salto was created in 1986 with the damming of the Elota River. The result is a remote reservoir that sprawls across 25,000 acres during the rainy months and 17,000 acres during the later portion of the bass season.

Its dreamland bass fishery bears the imprint of Billy Chapman Jr., owner of Anglers Inn International. Chapman and his father convinced the government to stock the fast growing Florida strain of largemouth into the Elota in 1985, a year before it was to be impounded for irrigation purposes. Billy later stocked about 2,000 fingerlings on his own.

Mexican authorities saw to it that those bass implants were left undisturbed for nearly five years. That allowed them to grow fat on shad and tilapia, which also were introduced by the government, he notes. By the time Chapman opened Anglers Inn in 1990, El Salto's largemouth population immediately lived up to his hopes and dreams. The lake quickly became renowned for its sheer abundance of bass — and as a place where 100-bass days occurred regularly.

But even a consummate dreamer like Chapman never

(Opposite page) TWO CASTS by these anglers produced a pair of 10-pounders from Lake El Salto.

envisioned the amazing bass lake that El Salto has become.

Those plentiful bass have obviously grown up. With a year-round growing season and a growth rate estimated by Mexican biologists at an unbelievable 2 pounds per year, an enormous crop of 7- to 14-pound bass now swim in these tropical waters. It has to be experienced to be believed.

"I really believe there are some 20-pound fish swimming in El Salto," Chapman states. "We found a 16 1/2-pounder floating near our dock with a tilapia stuck in its throat.

The big bass strategy on this lake involves big lures, rods and line. The most effective trophy lures include Fat Free Shad crankbaits, 10-inch Berkley Power Worms, soft plastic creatures like the Gambler Bacon Rind and Zoom Brush Hog, Heddon Zara Spook, Storm Big Bug chuggers and 3/4-ounce Terminator spinnerbaits.

Because much of the fishing occurs in centuries-old submerged mesquite trees and cactus, it is almost futile to use anything less than 20-pound-test line.

The best fishing action occurs in the upper half of the lake, where there are more than 30 islands, countless stands of flooded timber and the majority of El Salto's nearly 400 brush-covered points. Although the reservoir has some floating hyacinths, the flooded brush and trees seem to harbor the most bass and attract the most attention. And there are times when some of El Salto's more peculiar bass structure — the flooded ruins of two villages — gets hot.

Lake El Salto provides a fishing trip that is perfect for families. Accommodations at Chapman's Anglers Inn lakeside lodge are first class. The fishing takes place in stable, comfortable boats with guides that speak at least some English, and the bass are usually big and cooperative.

LAKE COMEDERO

The story of Lake Comedero's transformation from a "numbers" bass lake into a trophy fishery is an easy one to understand. Renowned outfitter Ron Speed opened his camp there in the village of Higueres de Urrea in 1988, a year after he put 60,000 Florida bass fingerlings in the impoundment. Originally stocked with northern-strain largemouth by the Mexican government in 1984, Comedero quickly became one of those famous "100 bass per day" Mexican lakes.

Thousands of anglers from throughout the United States flew south to Comedero for three and four day trips. Comedero bass were seldom heavier than 6 pounds, but there were so many of them no one cared about trophies. In 1988, Speed took 70 trophy largemouth, including fish to 10 pounds, from El Salto and stocked them in Comedero.

The next year, he put 120,000 more pure Florida fingerlings into Comedero's deep, clear waters, and in 1990, he chartered an aircraft and flew 100,000 more to the lake.

By May 1994, however, a combination of drought and other conditions began to slow the fishing dramatically. When the action dropped below Speed's personal minimum of 50 bass per day per angler, he closed his camp at Comedero.

By 1996, however, more and more stories of

LUNKER HUNTERS from the states would be remiss if they missed out on the four-star accommodations Mexico has to offer: Baccarac, Comedero, El Salto and Aguamilpa.

big bass being caught at the 27,000-acre lake began circulating. A number of anglers were trailering their own boats to Comedero, but Speed didn't pay much attention to the stories because most were of bass in the 8- to 10-pound range.

Then came the rumor of a commercial fisherman who claimed to have caught two 18-pounders from Comedero. Speed sent his Mazatlan-based Mexican manager, Carlos Lizarraga, to Comedero to see what he could find out, and also to fish the lake. Carlos found the commercial angler, who had shared his catch with the townsfolk in a huge fish fry, and went fishing with him. It was a dreary, rainy day and they only fished six hours, but during that time they landed one bass weighing 10 1/2 pounds, another over 8 and two over 7 pounds. All came on a Pop-R, Carlos' favorite lure.

The next day, they went out again, and Carlos lost the Pop-R and much of his line to a giant bass he never turned.

Then came another report — that another commercial angler had brought in a 10-kilo bass — a 22-pounder. If that were true, Comedero might easily hold a world record largemouth. Lizarraga and Speed both talked to the butcher who reportedly had weighed the bass, but of course by that time the fish had long since been cut up and sold.

It was only after one of his former guides made the long bus trip to Carlos' home in Mazatlan to tell him about a big bass, that Speed realized the potential magnitude of the Comedero fishery.

While sitting in Carlos' living room, the guide, a teen-age boy named Francisco, described in detail catching a 22-pound bass on a hand line. Speed and Carlos both knew and respected the boy, who had guided for them in the past. More importantly, in a country where 20-pound bass simply mean more food to eat, this young angler at least realized how important such a fish was to his employers.

"At that point, we knew without a doubt that Comedero was holding some huge bass," recalls Speed. "The story Francisco told us had real credibility, because we knew him as one of our better guides. When we combined his story with all the others of lost fish we were getting from our own clients, we knew it would only be a matter of time before one of those fish was put in the boat."

LAKE AGUAMILPA

It may be the best Mexican bass lake you've never heard of. And that puts it among the very best bass waters in the world.

After a half-mile or so of driving along concrete walls that support a gleaming white dam, your senses are suddenly delighted by the appearance of Aguamilpa, a sparkling, aqua-colored pool that resembles an exotic movie set. It has to rank among the most picturesque bass habitat in existence.

ONE OF THE most scenic lakes in Mexico, Aguamilpa is a terrific backdrop for trophy bass fishing.

BECAUSE THEY LIVE
in warm water year-round, the metabolism of Mexican bass remains high and as a result, they have voracious appetites.

But there is much more to Aguamilpa than just its good looks and charm. Belying its sheer beauty is a bruiser of a bass fishery. You might not be aware of it, but Aguamilpa deserves to be rated as the best numbers lake south of the border. And these numbers have some size to them. To fish Lake Milpa is to be impressed with both the consistent action and average quality size of the combatants.

This wonderful waterway had been in the minds of Mexican officials back in the 1950s, as they dreamed of constructing a large hydroelectric power reservoir in the coastal state of Nayarit. It took 40 years to act on their plans, but construction began in the early 1990s in this rugged region of the Sierra Madre mountains.

By 1994, the Aguamilpa Dam had been completed, successfully blocking the Santiago, Lerma and Rafael rivers and creating a sprawling 70,000-acre lake that, from the air, resembles a large wishbone. Upon completion, the nearly 70-mile-long lake engulfed two major mountain drainages below the Sierra Madre Occidental and inundated about 330 miles of shoreline. Its maximum depth is 650 feet.

The result is one of the most amazing backdrops a bass angler could ever hope to experience. Located at an elevation of more than 2,600 feet above sea level, Aguamilpa is home to colorful parrots and other exotic creatures, as well as four beautiful waterfalls. And because of its elevation, pesky insects are practically nonexistent, and the cool temperatures allow the typical Mexican bass season to extend through July.

From 1994 to '97, Lake Milpa was closed to fishing. But during that time, a promising largemouth fishery was brewing, thanks to the vision of Billy Chapman Sr. Chapman, the dean of Mexican outfitters with more than 35 years' experience in trade, stocked more than 500 Florida-strain bass in holding tanks that would eventually be flooded.

Today, visitors are enjoying the fruits of his foresight.

With a growth rate estimated by Mexican biologists at 2 pounds per year, Lake Milpa's bass population gets noticeably bigger each season. Consider that the record for this young lake is already 12 1/2 pounds.

But it is the mind-boggling abundance of quality bass swimming in these waters that remains the calling card of Aguamilpa. One-hundred-bass days are commonplace. And believe it or not, some customers have reported catching as many as 400 bass per boat in a single day.

"Of all of the lakes I've fished in Mexico, this is the best lake for numbers," says George Sanders of Colorado, who averaged 80 to 100 bass (up to 10 1/2 pounds) per day during a trip to Lake Milpa. "In my opinion, it's the best lake for action."

A large part of the beauty of fishing Aguamilpa is the ability to catch good numbers of fish on just about any lure. A fisherman who enjoys power fishing with crankbaits, spinnerbaits and jerkbaits can collect dozens of bass in a day's time. Topwater enthusiasts usually enjoy the kind of nonstop

action seldom found in the United States. And the more finesse-oriented anglers can simply mop up with plastic worms and other soft creatures.

The fishing season on Aguamilpa is Oct. 15 to July 15. Since its water is used for hydroelectric power purposes, Aguamilpa rarely experiences the major fluctuations during the season that hamper other Mexican lakes.

Chapman, in conjunction with son and fellow outfitter Billy Chapman Jr., operates the only outfitting service on the lake. The Chapman-Balderama Lodge was built on a cliffside plateau, where it has a spectacular view of the lake and dam.

LAKE BACCARAC

All the big bass tales emanating from Mexico in recent years must make it difficult for fishermen to separate fact from fiction. But statistics don't lie, and the numbers prove that Lake Baccarac has become one of the premier trophy bass fisheries of Mexico.

"I think there is a world record in there," claims longtime guide Felipe Valdez. Baccarac has produced three fish in the 19-pound class, including the lake record catch of 19 pounds, 10 ounces. Valdez believes some huge bass in the deep waters of Baccarac have never seen a lure, since most anglers fish shallow there.

Baccarac's age, structure and depth are all key factors in producing its big bass. The 19-year-old lake was originally stocked with Florida-strain largemouth, which have had plenty of time to grow huge and produce trophy-size offspring as well.

"This was the first lake in Mexico stocked with pure Florida-strain bass," claims Valdez. The warm climate allows Baccarac bass to grow year-round at an annual rate of 1 1/2 to 2 pounds.

Fed by the Sinaloa River, Baccarac's waters spread to about 35,000 acres when full and about 28,000 acres at its lowest level. The impoundment has a maximum depth of about 200 feet. Valdez believes the lake's deep water helps retain its big bass population. "Those big fish don't eat all the time, and they don't have to move shallow to eat,"

he says. "If the tilapia (a favorite forage of Baccarac bass) are in 20 feet of water, the bass will eat there."

The cover and structure also vary with the changing lake level. "This lake has everything — deep water, shallow water, flats, ledges, dropoffs, islands, creeks, rocks and wood," says Valdez. Baccarac contains 76 to 96 islands — depending on the water level — and plenty of standing timber, even at its lowest level. Shoreline bushes and trees become inundated when the lake level rises.

Valdez rates December through March as the peak months to fish Baccarac. December is a prime time to throw any type of crankbait in the same hues (black and silver, green and pearl) as baby bass, shad or tilapia.

January is a prime month for throwing topwaters at Baccarac. The best lures for trophy fish are Rebel Pop-Rs, Strike King Spit'n Kings and Heddon Zara Spooks with black backs and chrome sides.

A variety of lures produce bass in February and March. Some favorites for trophy fish include chartreuse or white spinnerbaits, Slug-Gos, Zoom Flukes, Berkley Power Jerks in pearl-white or gray shad, black or white Yamamoto Senkos and 8-inch plastic grubs and lizards (in tequila sunrise, black and blue, black and chartreuse or red shad). During our trip in early March, most of the big fish were taken on black Senkos and white spinnerbaits.

A lack of fishing pressure also greatly enhances the chances of catching a double-digit bass. Baccarac Lodge is the only fishing camp on this remote lake nestled in the Sierra Madre Mountains. "We only operate from October through March or the first of April," says Valdez. "So the rest of the year, nobody fishes it."

The resort manager estimates only 20 boats are on the lake each day, even during peak times. Ten boats were the most on the lake at one time during my stay. The average number of boats per day throughout the season is 15.

Here you have hundreds of trophy bass and fewer than two dozen anglers to fish for them at one time. Those Baccarac numbers are the kinds of odds any Bassmaster would love to play.

U.S. BASS RECORDS
Check this list to set your mark for breaking a record

SPECIES	WEIGHT	YEAR, LOCATION
Alabama		
Largemouth	16 lbs., 8 ozs.	1987, Mountain View Lake
Redeye	3 lbs., 2 ozs.	2000, Choccolocco Creek
Shoal	6 lbs., 11 ozs.	1996, Halawakee Creek
Smallmouth	10 lbs., 8 ozs.	1950, Wheeler Dam tailwaters
Spotted	8 lbs., 15 ozs.	1978, Lewis Smith Lake
Arizona		
Largemouth	16 lbs., 14 ozs.	1996, Colorado River
Smallmouth	7 lbs., 0.96 oz.	1988, Roosevelt Lake
Arkansas		
Largemouth	16 lbs., 4 ozs.	1976, Lake Mallard
Smallmouth	7 lbs., 5 ozs.	1969, Bull Shoals Lake
Spotted	7 lbs., 15 ozs.	1983, Bull Shoals Lake
California		
Largemouth	21 lbs., 1.92 ozs.	1991, Lake Castaic
Smallmouth	9 lbs., 1.6 ozs.	1976, Clair Engle Lake
Spotted	10 lbs., 4 ozs.	2001, Pine Flat Reservoir
Colorado		
Largemouth	11 lbs., 6 ozs.	1997, Echo Canyon Reservoir
Smallmouth	5 lbs., 12 ozs.	1993, Navajo Reservoir
Spotted	2 lbs., 17 ozs.	1996, Pueblo Reservoir
Connecticut		
Largemouth	12 lbs., 14 ozs.	1961, Mashapaug Lake
Smallmouth	7 lbs., 12 ozs.	1980, Shenipsit Lake
Delaware		
Largemouth	10 lbs., 5 ozs.	1980, Andrews Lake
Smallmouth	4 lbs., 15.5 ozs.	1989, Brandywine River
Florida		
Largemouth	20 lbs., 2.08 ozs.	1923, Big Fish Lake
Redeye	7 lbs., 13.28 ozs.	1989, Apalachicola River
Spotted	3 lbs., 12 ozs.	1985, Apalachicola River
Suwannee	3 lbs., 14.24 ozs.	1985, Suwannee River
Georgia		
Largemouth	22 lbs., 4 ozs.	1932, Montgomery Lake
Redeye	3 lbs., 5 ozs.	1999, Lake Hartwell
Shoal	8 lbs., 3 ozs.	1977, Flint River
Smallmouth	7 lbs., 2 ozs.	1973, Lake Chatuge
Spotted	8 lbs., 0.5 oz.	1985, Lake Lanier
Suwannee	3 lbs., 9 ozs.	1984, Ochlocknee River

SPECIES	WEIGHT	YEAR, LOCATION
Hawaii		
Largemouth	9 lbs., 9.4 ozs.	1992, Waita Reservoir
Peacock	9 lbs., 6.72 ozs.	1990, Lihue
Smallmouth	2 lbs., 9.6 ozs.	1979, Lake Wilson
Idaho		
Largemouth	10 lbs., 15 ozs.	prior to 1962, Anderson Lake
Smallmouth	8 lbs., 5 ozs.	1995, Dworshak Reservoir
Illinois		
Largemouth	13 lbs., 1 oz.	1976, Stone Quarry Lake
Smallmouth	6 lbs., 7 ozs.	1985, strip mine
Spotted	7 lbs., 3.12 ozs.	1992, strip mine
Indiana		
Largemouth	14 lbs., 12 ozs.	1991, lake in Harrison County
Smallmouth	7 lbs., 4 ozs.	1992, Twin Lake
Spotted	5 lbs., 1.5 ozs.	1975, lake in Howard County
Iowa		
Largemouth	10 lbs., 14 ozs.	1984, Lake Fisher
Smallmouth	7 lbs., 12 ozs.	1990, Spirit Lake
Kansas		
Largemouth	11 lbs., 12 ozs.	1977, farm pond
Smallmouth	6 lbs., 5.92 ozs.	1997, Milford Reservoir
Spotted	4 lbs., 7 ozs.	1977, Marion County Lake
Kentucky		
Largemouth	13 lbs., 10.4 ozs.	1984, Woods Creek Lake
Smallmouth	8 lbs., 7.36 ozs.	1998, Laurel River Lake
Spotted	7 lbs., 10 ozs.	1970, Nelson County Water
Louisiana		
Largemouth	15 lbs., 15.52 ozs.	1994, Caney Lake
Spotted	4 lbs., 14.08 ozs.	1976, Tickfaw River
Maine		
Largemouth	11 lbs., 10 ozs.	1968, Moose Pond
Smallmouth	8 lbs., 0 ozs.	1970, Thompson Lake
Maryland		
Largemouth	11 lbs., 2 ozs.	1983, farm pond
Smallmouth	8 lbs., 4 ozs.	1974, Liberty Reservoir
Massachusetts		
Largemouth	15 lbs., 8 ozs.	1975, Sampson's Pond
Smallmouth	8 lbs., 2 ozs.	1991, Wachusett Reservoir

SPECIES	WEIGHT	YEAR, LOCATION
Michigan		
Largemouth	11 lbs., 15.04 ozs.	1934, Pine Island Lake; 1959, Bamfield Dam (tie)
Smallmouth	9 lbs., 4 ozs.	1906, Long Lake
Minnesota		
Largemouth	8 lbs., 12.75 ozs.	1994, Lake TeTonka
Smallmouth	8 lbs., 0 ozs.	1949, West Battle Lake
Mississippi		
Largemouth	18 lbs., 2.4 ozs.	1992, Natchez State Park Lake
Smallmouth	7 lbs., 15 ozs.	1987, Pickwick Lake
Spotted	8 lbs., 2 ozs.	1975, farm pond
Missouri		
Largemouth	13 lbs., 14 ozs.	1961, Bull Shoals
Smallmouth	7 lbs., 2 ozs.	1994, Stockton Lake
Spotted	7 lbs., 8 ozs.	1966, Table Rock Lake
Montana		
Largemouth	8 lbs., 4.64 ozs.	1999, Many Lakes
Smallmouth	6 lbs., 10.56 ozs.	2002, Fort Peck Reservoir
Nebraska		
Largemouth	10 lbs., 11 ozs.	1965, sandpit
Smallmouth	7 lbs., 4 ozs.	2000, Missouri River
Spotted	3 lbs., 12 ozs.	1990, sandpit
Nevada		
Largemouth	12 lbs., 0 ozs.	1999, Lake Mead
Smallmouth	5 lbs., 7 ozs.	2001, South Fork Reservoir
Spotted	4 lbs., 2 ozs.	2000, Rye Patch Reservoir
New Hampshire		
Largemouth	10 lbs., 8 ozs.	1967, Lake Potanipo
Smallmouth	7 lbs., 14.5 ozs.	1970, Goose Pond
New Jersey		
Largemouth	10 lbs., 14 ozs.	1980, Menantico Sand Wash Pond
Smallmouth	7 lbs., 2 ozs.	1990, Round Valley Reservoir
New Mexico		
Largemouth	15 lbs., 13 ozs.	1995, Bill Evans Lake
Smallmouth	6 lbs., 14.4 ozs.	1999, Navajo Lake
Spotted	4 lbs., 8 ozs.	1988, Cochiti Lake
New York		
Largemouth	11 lbs., 4 ozs.	1987, Buckhorn Lake
Smallmouth	8 lbs., 4 ozs.	1995, Lake Erie

State/Nation Where Lunkers Were Caught

Lakes With Most Lunker Club Catches

State/Nation	Percentage Of Catches
Florida	26.6
Texas	18.7
California	16.2
Mexico	6.1
Arizona	4.0
Georgia	4.0
Louisiana	4.0
Alabama	2.9
Mississippi	2.9
North Carolina	2.9
Virginia	2.2
Oklahoma	1.4
South Carolina	1.4

Lake	Number Of Catches
Lake Fork, Texas	30
Small Ponds	27
Lake Guerrero, Mexico	11
Clear Lake, Calif.	9
Lake Walk-In-Water, Fla.	9
Stick Marsh/Farm 13, Fla.	6
Istokpoga, Fla.	6

(States and nations with fewer than three Lunker Club catches: South Africa, Arkansas, Tennessee, Delaware, Illinois, Indiana, Missouri, Nevada, Ohio, Oregon and Utah.)

SPECIES	WEIGHT	YEAR, LOCATION
North Carolina		
Largemouth	15 lbs., 14 ozs.	1991, farm pond
Smallmouth	10 lbs., 2 ozs.	1951, Hiwassee Reservoir
Spotted	5 lbs., 15 ozs.	1992, Lake Chatuge
North Dakota		
Largemouth	8 lbs., 7.5 ozs.	1983, Nelson Lake
Smallmouth	5 lbs., 9 ozs.	1999, Sakakawea
Ohio		
Largemouth	13 lbs., 2.08 ozs.	1976, farm pond
Smallmouth	9 lbs., 8 ozs.	1993, Lake Erie
Spotted	5 lbs., 4 ozs.	1976, Lake White
Oklahoma		
Largemouth	14 lbs., 11.52 ozs.	1999, Broken Bow Lake
Smallmouth	7 lbs., 8 ozs.	1996, Lake Texoma
Spotted	8 lbs., 2 ozs.	1958, Pittsburg County pond
Oregon		
Largemouth	12 lbs., 1.6 ozs.	2002, Ballenger Pond
Smallmouth	7 lbs., 14 ozs.	2000, Henry Hagg Lake
Pennsylvania		
Largemouth	11 lbs., 3 ozs.	1983, Birch Run Reservoir
Smallmouth	8 lbs., 8 ozs.	1997, Scotts Run Lake
Rhode Island		
Largemouth	10 lbs., 6 ozs.	1991, Carbuncle Pond
Smallmouth	5 lbs., 15 ozs.	1977, Wash Pond
South Carolina		
Largemouth	16 lbs., 2 ozs.	1949, Lake Marion; 1993, Aiken County pond (tie)
Redeye	5 lbs., 2.5 ozs.	2001, Lake Jocassee
Smallmouth	9 lbs., 7 ozs.	2001, Lake Jocassee
Spotted	8 lbs., 5 ozs.	2001, Lake Jocassee
South Dakota		
Largemouth	9 lbs., 3 ozs.	1999, Hudson Gravel Pit
Smallmouth	6 lbs., 2 ozs.	1999, Lewis & Clark Lake

SPECIES	WEIGHT	YEAR, LOCATION
Tennessee		
Largemouth	14 lbs., 8 ozs.	1954, Sugar Creek
Redeye	1 lb., 14.5 ozs.	1991, Parksville Reservoir
Smallmouth	11 lbs., 15 ozs.	1955, Dale Hollow Reservoir
Spotted	5 lbs., 8 ozs.	1989, Center Hill Lake
Texas		
Guadalupe	3 lbs., 11.04 ozs.	1983, Lake Travis
Largemouth	18 lbs., 2.88 ozs.	1992, Lake Fork
Smallmouth	7 lbs., 14.88 ozs.	1998, Meredith
Spotted	5 lbs., 8. ozs.	1966, Lake O' The Pines
Utah		
Largemouth	10 lbs., 2 ozs.	1974, Lake Powell
Smallmouth	7 lbs., 6 ozs.	1996, Midview Reservoir
Vermont		
Largemouth	10 lbs., 4 ozs.	1988, Lake Dunmore
Smallmouth	6 lbs., 12 ozs.	1978, Lake Champlain
Virginia		
Largemouth	16 lbs., 4 ozs.	1985, Lake Conner
Smallmouth	7 lbs., 7 ozs.	1986, New River
Spotted	3 lbs., 10 ozs.	1993, Claytor Lake
Washington		
Largemouth	11 lbs., 9.12 ozs.	1977, Banks Lake
Smallmouth	8 lbs., 13.92 ozs.	1966, Columbia River
West Virginia		
Largemouth	12 lbs., 4.48 ozs.	1994, pond
Smallmouth	9 lbs., 12 ozs.	1971, South Branch
Spotted	4 lbs., 12.32 ozs.	2000, R.D. Bailey Lake
Wisconsin		
Largemouth	11 lbs., 3 ozs.	1940, Lake Ripley
Smallmouth	9 lbs., 1 oz.	1950, Indian Lake
Wyoming		
Largemouth	7 lbs., 14 ozs.	1992, Girl's School Pond
Smallmouth	5 lbs., 1.28 ozs.	1993, Tongue River

FOR A TRUE test of sport, try for a lunker on the fly.

Sources: National Fresh Water Fishing Hall of Fame and various state fisheries agencies

THE RECORD LARGEMOUTH

Will the record ever be broken?

THE WORLD RECORD LARGEMOUTH was caught on this Creek Chub 2401-W (wooden) Wiggle Fish in perch-scale pattern.

THE WORLD RECORD BASS

In more than 70 years, many have tried, but not one has succeeded in catching the biggest bass of all time

BASS, Largemouth (*Micropterus salmoides*) — 22 pounds, 4 ounces — Montgomery Lake, Ga., United States — June 2, 1932 — George W. Perry

COMPETITIVE FISHING HAS CHANGED the way millions of Americans fish. Bass clubs sprang up, with weekend anglers striving to emulate their new heroes: Tom Mann and Bill Dance and Roland Martin. Exciting new boats, motors, tackle and electronics were introduced as the BASS trail became a research and development lab, torture-testing the hardware everyday fishermen would soon be using. For many, the focus of the sport gradually shifted away from big bass.

Over the years, George W. Perry and his world record bass became a quaint sidebar in the annals of bass angling, rather like Casey Jones would be in a discussion of modern railroading. As the years melted into decades, Perry's feat became more unapproachable.

Big bass were caught by other anglers, but none that could begin to compare with the one landed that June day in 1932. Too much fishing pressure and too little regard for the resource dramatically depleted the supply of big bass. The rapid spread of industry and the movement of great numbers of people into previously unsettled areas caused a decline in bass habitat. Big bass became a rarity, a curiosity.

Fewer people could justify devoting their precious fishing time to hunting that solitary lunker. Beating Perry's record seemed as improbable as lassoing the moon.

Then news of a giant bass — a fish bigger than anything we'd seen or heard about since Perry's day — came from the West. California, of all places, produced an enormous fish, a fortuitous blending of fisheries management and fate. Dave Zimmerlee caught a 20-pound, 15-ounce bass from Lake Miramar in 1973, a potbellied, bug-eyed Florida hybrid that stunned the angling world and offered a new ray of hope to those who thought Perry's record unbeatable. For a time, the bass anglers of America refocused on big fish.

(Opposite page) NO ANGLER has matched the feat of George W. Perry, who caught the world record largemouth in 1932.

Other massive California bass followed, but it was a full seven years before another 20-plus was taken. In 1980, Ray Easley boated a 21-pound, 3-ounce bass from Lake Casitas, and the Golden State's bid for the record books loomed imminent.

The big fish bug bit hard, and California lakes containing the massive Florida hybrids received unrelenting fishing pressure. The outdoor media speculated that it was only a matter of months before somebody would crack the Holy Grail of angling records and find his or her name replacing Perry's in the record books. But the decade of the '80s proved disappointing, with only one more bass, a 20-4 caught in '85 from Lake Hodges, topping the 20-pound barrier. Many felt California's chance had come and gone. Like the carnival barker at the ring-toss game told me as he pocketed my quarter, "Close . . . but no cigar!"

Then came the '90s, and an unprecedented wave of giant California bass. Bob Crupi caught a 21-pounder from Lake Castaic in '90, and followed it up with a 22-pounder in '91, making the Los Angeles motorcycle policeman the only human to have boated two verified largemouth black bass over 20 pounds. His 22 (actually 22.01

NO ONE KNOWS when or where the next world record will be broken. The question is, after more than 70 years will it ever be broken?

pounds) is currently the second-biggest largemouth ever documented. Crupi released the fish into Lake Castaic. Two other California anglers would boat 20-something-pound bass before the dawn of the 21st century: Leo Torres (20-14) and Mike Arujo (21-12), both from Castaic.

Suddenly Perry's fish seems within reach, and this conjures up mixed emotions among avid bass fishermen nationwide. Many regard George W. Perry and his bass as treasured facets of bass angling's rich heritage, and would like to see 22-4 emblazoned forever in the annals of sportfishing. Others believe the time has come for a new world record, and anxiously await the word that someone, somewhere, has finally done the deed. While competitive fishing continues to have a major presence in the world of the bass, big fish are indeed big news once again.

DREAM QUEST

Giant bass have captivated many fishermen, including Doug Hannon, Florida's famous "Bass Professor." The big bass authority has caught over 500 largemouth exceeding 10 pounds apiece, and has made the pursuit of big bass his life's goal. "There's no question that George Perry's bass had a profound impact on my life," he said. "I read and reread the various accounts of the catch. As an adult, I tried for years to catch a bass bigger than Perry's."

Hannon, whose biggest bass is a 17-pounder, explained that record-hunting is a different kind of bass fishing.

"There's nothing relaxing about it. It becomes a burning compulsion," he said. "It's a quest that has been the ruination of many a fisherman. Back when I was seriously hunting a record, I'd cross paths with others who were searching for that same pot of gold. One was a millionaire insurance executive who had cashed it all in — he was totally possessed by the dream of beating Perry's fish. Another was a grizzled old guide who swore he'd seen it, and burnt himself out trying to catch it.

"Record-hunting is a lonely proposition. But it made me realize just how special big bass really are, and how extraordinary a world record is."

DAVE ZIMMERLEE'S 20-5 monster from Lake Miramar in 1973 launched the modern day world record chase.

Hannon's quest for information about giant bass led him to old books and manuscripts, many detailing early expeditions into Florida's vast wilderness areas.

"I read a chronicle about an expedition by a doctor and his party at the turn of the century, a journey they made into the Everglades," he said. "These were learned men, broad-based in the natural sciences and not accustomed to fouling up weights and measurements."

Hannon read with amazement that one of the explorers caught a largemouth bass that weighed 26 pounds and had a length of 34 inches and a girth of 28 3/4 inches.

"The doctor included in his account complete measurements of the distance between eyes and mandible and other detailed information. Based on the formula: length x length x length divided by 1600 = estimated weight, 26 pounds seemed very accurate. Besides, why would a group of explorers lie about a big bass back in 1900, when they had nothing to gain from it? For all they knew, fish that big were common."

The story of the Everglades explorers gave Hannon a ray of hope through his record-hunting years. "I felt that if there had been a 26-pounder, then it was possible to believe that a 22-6 would still exist. (That's how big a largemouth must be to beat Perry's record under IGFA rules.) And

(Opposite page) FLORIDA TROPHY expert Doug Hannon believes Florida's chances of producing a new world record are slim due to overdevelopment.

BOB CRUPI is the only angler to catch more than one largemouth weighing over 20 pounds, including this monster weighing 22-01.

when you're after that one fish, hope is sometimes all you have going for you."

Hannon believes Florida's chances of producing a world record largemouth are slim today. "The state has allowed its lakes and rivers to be fished out through their antiquated laws and unrealistic bag limits. Here, bed fishing is an industry. You used to see 500, maybe 1,000 bass beds in some of our lakes, but not any more. The fishing was so incredible when I came here in 1970, you could catch seven or eight 10-pounders in a single day.

"I caught many huge bass, some over 15 pounds. It was inconceivable back then that there weren't hundreds of world record bass swimming in the state. Now you go up into some of those remote rivers and small lakes and the shoreline is ringed with condominiums and shopping centers."

Like most anglers today, Hannon believes California has the best shot at a world record.

"There's a group of guys — Bob Crupi, Danny Kadota, Bill Murphy — who are out there gunning for it right now," he said. "They're not millionaires

with time on their hands; they don't have TV shows and 25 different product endorsements. They're doing it for the love of the quest. This is the essence of record-hunting. It's the dream that keeps you going."

A certified world record largemouth has been touted by the outdoor press as being worth upward of $1 million to the angler fortunate enough to catch it — quite a leap from Perry's day, when the most that could be gleaned from the catch was a shotgun and some lures.

"The fish will be worth far more alive than as a mounted trophy," Hannon said. "This may raise some ethical questions for the fisherman who catches it. For example, a large corporation may want to buy the fish to exhibit it, or use in some sort of promotion. It's a different climate today than before. Who knows what problems and controversy might arise?"

Whoever catches the record has another option: releasing the bass. "Can you imagine the impact this would have on the angling world, the statement it would make about conservation?" he suggests.

Hannon feels that while Perry's bass will always hold a special place in the history of the sport. A new world record could have important benefits to the future of bass fishing.

"It would put big fish back in their proper perspective, and showcase them for the amazing creatures they are. Plus, many fishermen make their decision to keep a 5-, 6- or 10-pound bass on their assumption that there's no real hope that the fish might grow to be a giant someday. A new world record might open their eyes to the value of releasing big bass. They might realize that the fish they hold in their hands could someday be a giant."

CALIFORNIA ANGLER Leaha Trew says her trophy bass weighed at least 22 pounds, 8 ounces. She released the fish before a biologist could verify the weight.

A Challenge To The World Record?

Is the name, Spring Lake, Calif., familiar? If you're a student of record class largemouth bass, you'll remember the giant bass Paul Duclos caught from the 75-acre lake near Santa Rosa on March 1, 1997. Duclos weighed his fish on bathroom scales and then released it, forever leaving in doubt whether it actually did weigh 24 pounds, as he stated.

More recently, Santa Rosa, Calif., angler Leaha Trew claimed she, too, caught a giant bass from Spring Lake, this one reportedly weighing 22 pounds, 8 ounces. It, too, was released before officials could examine it. According to her son, Javad, who was fishing with her at the time of the catch, the bass was weighed on handheld scales that previously had been certified for accuracy. The pair submitted applications for largemouth bass world record status to the International Game Fish Association (IGFA) and the National Fresh Water Fishing Hall of Fame.

According to the application, the bass measured 29 inches in length and had a girth of 25 inches. It was caught Aug. 24, 2003, on a Storm Wildeye Jerkbait.

Had it been certified, the Spring Lake bass would surpass the all-tackle world record of 22 pounds, 4 ounces, caught by George W. Perry in Montgomery Lake, Ga., on June 2, 1932. Perry's bass was 32 inches long and 28 inches in girth.

William Cox, an employee of the California Department of Fish & Game who oversees the management of Spring Lake, said he signed the angler's application to the Fishing Hall of Fame, but he did not personally see the fish. Nor can he verify that the angler actually caught the bass in question, or that the fish was even caught in Spring Lake.

"If (the angler) had brought the fish to me, and I had been able to verify the weight and that it came from Spring Lake, it probably would be accepted as the world record," says Cox. "I can only verify that I saw a photograph of the bass and that it was big."

Noting that Javad Trew "is an experienced angler who has several other line class records (including an 18 1/2-pounder he caught from Spring Lake a month later)," Cox added, "He should have made some effort to keep the fish for examination, since Spring Lake is not a catch-and-release lake." Javad says he now regrets that he and his mother did not keep the fish.

Because a biologist did not inspect the fish, the Fresh Water Fishing Hall of Fame would not certify it as the world record, although the Hall did accept it as a line class record and declared it the "unofficial world record."

The other records-keeping organization, IGFA, also has stringent requirements for the world record, and it does not have an "unofficial" category. Noting that "there are several significant omissions in her application," the four-person IGFA Record Confirmation Committee denied the Trew fish world record status.

A photo of Trew and her fish (shown at left) convinced a number of experts at judging trophy bass that the fish did not weigh 22-8. Using the widely accepted formula for estimating weight — length times length times girth divided by 1200 — the bass would weigh about 17 1/2 pounds. Since the bass was released so quickly, the world will never know for sure.

RETURN TO MONTGOMERY LAKE
A pilgrimage to the former 'home' of the world record

THE YEAR: 1932. Times were tough in south Georgia. And George W. Perry, a 19-year-old farm boy, had a job to do.

He was going fishing. Not for fun, but for food. The Great Depression held a death grip on the country, and down Georgia way, if you didn't grow it, trap it, or catch it . . . very often you went hungry.

The season for bass had just opened (yes, Georgia had a bass season back in '32) and Perry knew where to go to catch a mess of "green trout," as largemouth bass were called back then. He headed for the Ocmulgee River, putting in at Lumber City.

Seven fruitless miles of casting later, George W. Perry made what was to become a very big

Perry And His Bass

The facts surrounding George Perry's world record bass have become fogged through 60 years of retelling. Augusta, Ga., outdoor journalist Bill Baab is considered by many to be the foremost authority on Perry and his fish. He interviewed Perry and members of his family, and has spent years digging into the facts of what transpired on Montgomery Lake six decades ago.

According to Baab, George Perry was 20 years old when the events took place that would forever change the world of bass fishing. "On June 2, 1932, it was raining when Perry woke up. That meant he couldn't go into the fields to plow or plant, so he decided to go fishing instead. Perry and a friend, Jack Page, drove to Montgomery Lake, leaving before daylight in Page's truck. Perry kept a homemade flatbottom boat at the lake."

A 1934 account published in *Field & Stream* provides some titillating details of what happened next. According to author Seth Briggs, Perry and Page pounded the water without success, then talked about calling it quits. On their way back to the landing, Perry had a fair strike, but didn't connect. He kept on casting and was just about to give up when he noticed "an interesting ripple" near a cypress log.

The pair rowed closer. Perry made a long cast, and the bass struck. "I got just what I'd been looking for all morning," Perry was quoted as saying. "I knew at once that I was fast into a real bass. After playing him for about two minutes, I brought him close to the boat. Suddenly, he jumped almost clear of the water. I had a good look at him, and it seemed as though he ought to weigh about 50 pounds. He made for an old treetop, and I knew if he reached there, it would be just too bad. I tightened down on the spool with my thumb and succeeded in turning him just before he reached the tree. Finally, he gave up the fight and I reeled him up to the boat. After I had brought him into the boat, we began making wild guesses as to what he would weigh . . . we started back without even making another cast."

Baab said that one account indicated Perry was using his lure, later identified as a Creek Chub 2401-W (wooden) Wiggle Fish in perch-scale pattern, as a topwater plug, twitching it on the surface with his rod tip. The Wiggle Fish was designed to be used as a diver, and was equipped with a metal lip. "Perry's son recalled that his father had only one rod, one reel and two lures on the date the fish was caught," Baab said.

Perry and Page took the bass to a small grocery store in nearby Helena, where it was weighed. But Perry had no inkling that this bass was the largest ever certified. The International Game Fish Association (IGFA), official keeper of fresh- and saltwater world record gamefish, wouldn't exist for another seven years. "But somebody in the store mentioned the *Field & Stream* fishing contest, which was a popular fishing competition at the time," Baab said. "The magazine awarded merchandise annually for the winning fish in several categories, including bass."

Perry decided to enter his big bass in the contest. He took it to the Helena post office, where it was weighed on certified scales. The fish weighed 22 pounds, 4 ounces, measured 32 inches in length and had a 28-inch girth.

"Perry won the *Field & Stream* contest and received $75 in merchandise," Baab said. Prizes included a Browning automatic shotgun, some shells, fishing equipment and some outdoor clothing — a bonanza to a Georgia farm boy in the Depression. "Perry's sister told me how tickled George was when the prize package was delivered to their house," Baab recalled.

What became of Perry's fish? After fulfilling the contest rules, George did what you might expect any poor farmer to do at the time — he cleaned the fish, and his mother cooked it. It provided a meal for six family members.

GEORGE W. PERRY packed just two lures on his fateful trip to Lake Montgomery. One of them was this Creek Chub Wiggle Fish.

THE CREEK CHUB WIGGLE FISH used to catch the world record was the only bait that George W. Perry could afford at the time.

GEORGE W. PERRY had fished the Ocmulgee River without success before arriving at Montgomery Lake. His fate changed with one eventful cast.

decision. He decided to try an oxbow off the river known locally as "Montgomery Lake." Montgomery Lake could hardly be called a lake at all. It was a crescent-shaped pond, a mere slough. During times of high water, you could reach it quite easily from the Ocmulgee. When the water was down, you had to drag your boat in or walk in on foot . . . and watch for rattlesnakes every step of the way.

Perry fished Montgomery Lake that day, and caught more than a meal. He hooked and landed America's dream fish: the world record bass. A 22-pound, 4-ounce giant of a bass. A bass so big that the standard it set remains unmatched to this day.

Perry did it not with an arsenal of electronic gear, a high speed bass boat or a tacklebox full of baits. He owned but one fishing lure: a battered Creek Chub Wiggle Fish in the perch-scale pattern. His "kit" rod and reel would be the equivalent of a cheap outfit purchased at a discount store today.

Perhaps the fact that George Perry caught a world record bass — George Perry, a poor farm boy — makes this angling achievement all the more meaningful. For the largemouth bass is not the sportfish of aristocrats or kings — let them have their black marlin and bluefins. The bass is an everyday fish, for everyday people. And, like that Georgia farm boy back in '32, the bass is tenacious and tough. It doesn't give up easily. It's a fighter.

Former Bassmaster Classic champion Jack Chancellor represents a more modern ideal in the history of bass fishing: the successful tournament pro. It seemed fitting that, when *Bassmaster* sought to recreate Perry's record-breaking trip in words and photographs, Chancellor played the role of the record-holder.

A visit to Montgomery Lake is like stepping into a time warp. It represents everything that bass fishing used to be about before it was modernized by BASS in the late 1960s. Its size is the first indicator: The "lake" is barely bigger than many farm ponds. It's just an old oxbow off the Ocmulgee River, and, like all oxbows, it's slowly going back to the land. Someday, Montgomery Lake will be just an impression in the Georgia soil. The intensity of Perry's presence can be felt with every step closer that you take to the lake. It's magic — haunting to realize that history was made in this little old slough. A trip to this historical site is well worth the trouble for students of bass fishing history.

To reach Montgomery Lake, take Highway 117 from Jacksonville to Lumber City, Ga. Watch for a historical marker between the two towns, commemorating Perry's catch. Proceed toward Lumber City and watch for a sign indicating Highway 149 to your left. But instead of turning left, turn right onto a dirt road. Follow this road until you come to a paved ramp on the Ocmulgee River. During periods of heavy rainfall, you may need four-wheel drive to get that far.

Launch your boat in the Ocmulgee and head upriver. Watch for a clearing in the woods on your right about a quarter-mile past the ramp. Follow this trail a short distance, and there you'll find Montgomery Lake. You can walk in, or portage a lightweight boat with you. You'll want to travel light, like Perry did.

You can still catch some bass in Montgomery Lake, although most fishermen would rather fish someplace that's a little easier to get to. But if you go, don't go for the fishing.

Go for the memories.

WORLD RECORD BASS

Approximately two miles from this spot, on June 2, 1932, George W. Perry, a 19-year old farm boy, caught what was to become America's most famous fish. The twenty-two pound four ounce largemouth bass (Micropterus salmoides) exceeded the existing record by more than two pounds and has retained the world record for more than fifty years. Perry and his friend, J. E. Page, were fishing in Montgomery Lake, a slough off the Ocmulgee River, not for trophies but to bring food to the table during those days of the great depression. The fish was caught on a Creek Chub Perch Scale Wigglefish, Perry's only lure, and was 32½ inches in length and 28½ inches in girth. The weight and measurements were taken, recorded and notarized in Helena, Georgia. Perry's only reward was seventy-five dollars in merchandise as first prize in Field and Stream Magazine's fishing contest. The longstanding record is one of the reasons that the largemouth bass was made Georgia's Official State Fish. Montgomery Lake is today part of the Department of Natural Resources' Horse Creek Wildlife Management Area.

THIS MARKER STANDS near the site where history was made in the world of bass fishing.